The Swedish Acceptance
of American Literature

The Swedish Acceptance

of American Literature

by

CARL L. ANDERSON

PHILADELPHIA

UNIVERSITY OF PENNSYLVANIA PRESS

PRINTED IN SWEDEN BY

Almqvist & Wiksells

BOKTRYCKERI AKTIEBOLAG

UPPSALA 1957

To Jean

Contents

Preface

American literature is widely accepted in Europe today by critics and general readers alike, and the neglect and scorn that it endured only a few decades ago have already passed into history. In the years before World War I, American literature—except for a little of Cooper, Poe, Twain, and rarely one or two others—was virtually unknown to most European readers, and the existence of a literature worthy of the name had simply never seemed possible to most European critics. The beginnings of a radical change in opinion rapidly became apparent shortly after the Allied victory and Wilson's appearance in the role of international peacemaker and American intellectual. Nevertheless, the spectacular rise at that time of America's reputation in international affairs had no counterpart at first in literature and the arts. Translations were lacking, and so also were commentaries on the contemporary American writers who might have been expected by curious though still skeptical European readers to give insights into the bewildering life of the United States. Accordingly, a busy decade of translation and criticism followed. At its close in 1930, American literature had won at least the respect of the die-hards and very often the enthusiastic approval of other European critics. Obviously, whatever her shortcomings in this and other aspects of her culture, America could no longer be sweepingly dismissed as "culturally barren," "grossly materialistic," or incapable of fostering an exciting and independent literature.

It is the purpose of the pages that follow to offer a detailed account of this radical shift in the European attitude toward American literature as it occurred in one corner of the continent during the crucial, turbulent years between the end of World War I and 1930.

Sweden is an especially useful place to begin the study of the reputation of modern American literature in Europe. The smallness of the country has permitted students before this to look for a thoroughness seldom possible in studies of larger countries. At the same time Sweden offers in one country a wide range of literary opinion, which is usually sound though rarely distinguished. Finally, the award of the Swedish Nobel Prize in 1930 to an American writer dramatized, as did no other event elsewhere, the extent of the critical upheaval that had been taking place in Europe since the end of the war.

Ten years earlier, traditional prejudices against America would not have permitted any Swedish critic to suppose an award of the Prize to an American to be even remotely possible. The origin and force of these prejudices, therefore, deserve an important place in this account. They had long kept Swedish readers from giving more than a causal glance at American literature, either old or new; in the 1920's despite the new interest in America, they colored Swedish criticism of American literature; not until the award of the Prize to Sinclair Lewis were they abated (or sometimes replaced by others). It follows that the award of the Prize is the focal point of these chapters, and that their substance constitutes a history of Swedish criticism and book-reviewing with respect not only to Lewis's novels but also to those of his immediate predecessors, his contemporaries, and his successors. Together, these writers gave reality to the once fanciful concept called American literature.

Wherever possible and as far as my translations permit, the critics have been allowed to speak for themselves. The extensive use of newspaper reviews perhaps needs explanation. Every newspaper in Sweden entertains cultural pretensions that demand that the best available talent write its book reviews, if these are a regular part of the paper. The leading dailies of Stockholm, Göteborg, and Malmö, in addition to a few smaller ones, have therefore become a principal forum in Sweden for the discussion of literary topics. The contributors to these newspapers include Sweden's foremost critics, who write also for the journals and magazines but who not infrequently consider their best newspaper reviews worthy of collection in small volumes of criticism. Much, though by no means all, of the criticism cited in the following pages is taken from such newspaper reviews. However, since they are by the nature of their publication ephemeral and widely scattered, no pretense is made that every important piece of criticism of a particular book or author has been recovered. Enough has been nevertheless consulted to establish definite patterns and trends for our present purpose.

The labors of exhuming this criticism (which the newspapers do not index) were immeasurably lightened by my being kindly permitted by Mr. Bengt Hjelmqvist, head of the library section of Skolöverstyrelsen in Stockholm, to examine his department's little known but rich file of reviews. Taken chiefly from the 1915 to 1945 sections of this file, more than seven hundred reviews, notices, and other articles have been placed on microfilm along with essays and reviews from other sources, and the reels deposited in the Library of the University of Pennsylvania. Needless to say, not all this material is intrinsically valuable, some being brief notices useful only in corroborating or qualifying the trends in more important criticism. Only the more noteworthy, whether or not specifically referred to or quoted in the text, have been listed in a special bibliography in Appendix B. These may be said to constitute, with the material mentioned in the general bibliography, the basis for most of the text.

The backbone of such a study as this of the reception of American books in Sweden is of course the books themselves, and a complete list of American books of fiction published in Swedish translation from 1916 to 1945 is given in Appendix A. Although extending beyond the period discussed in the text, the full list is reproduced in order to give some indication of the activity after 1930.

Finally, Appendix C is a summary of the results of an extensive inquiry into the circulation of American books from twenty-two selected Swedish lending libraries. In so far as mere popularity of American fiction among the Swedish reading public bears upon the present issues, it would of course have been desirable to consult such a survey, or series of surveys, from the period 1920 to 1930. None having been undertaken then, however, recourse had to be made to this survey, which was completed in 1951. Whatever other merits it may have, it should dispel some erroneous impressions obtained in the past from a haphazard and meager sampling of lists of translations. Thanks for invaluable aid in planning the survey are due my friend Gösta Forsström, and once more Mr. Hjelmqvist, in addition to the staffs of the reporting libraries and Dr. Lars Åhnebrink, who gave his support to this and other matters.

In addition to those already mentioned, I am grateful, for advice and information, to the late Thorsten Jonsson, and to Dr. Anders Österling, Professor Gunnar Tideström, Dr. Gunnar Svanfeldt, Dr. Ivar Harrie, Dr. Harald Elovson, Mr. Åke Runnquist, Mrs. Britta Ersman, and Mr. Sven-Åke Svensson, all of Sweden; to Professor Sculley Bradley, for criticism and the opportunity to test some of the methods of this study in a seminar at the University of Pennsylvania; and to the authorities of the University of Pennsylvania and Sverige-Amerika Stiftelsen, and to Professor S. B. Liljegren, formerly of the University of Uppsala, for aid in making my stay in Sweden possible. Professor William L. Edgerton, Norwich University, read the final draft of the manuscript.

How far-reaching a debt I owe Professor Robert E. Spiller for precept and encouragement over many years I will not presume to say. His sure yet patient criticism has been an unfailing support.

To my friends, Björn and Brita Ahlander and Gösta Forsström, but most particularly to my wife, Jean Bradley Anderson, I owe much for practical assistance tendered always with heartwarming generosity.

C. L. A.

Durham, North Carolina.

List of Abbreviations Used

The most common newspaper sources cited in the text, bibliography, and appendixes are designated by the following abbreviations:

DN	*Dagens Nyheter* (Stockholm)
GHT	*Göteborgs Handels- och Sjöfarts-Tidning* (Göteborg)
NDA	*Nya Dagligt Allehanda* (Stockholm)
SDS	*Sydsvenska Dagbladet Snällposten* (Malmö)
Soc. Dem.	*Social-Demokraten* (Stockholm)
ST	*Stockholms-Tidningen* (Stockholm)
SvD	*Svenska Dagbladet* (Stockholm)

In addition, Henrik Schück and Karl Warburg, *Svensk litteraturhistoria,* VIII (by Erik Hj. Linder), Stockholm, 1949, is cited throughout as Schück—Warburg VIII.

CHAPTER I

The Swedish Animus Against American Literature

Inevitably, one result of the unmistakable emergence of the United States after World War I as a principal world power was that her literature should receive widespread, serious attention from European critics. The necessity imposed upon them by the outcome of the war to rediscover and reappraise "the great land in the west" was as strongly felt in Sweden as elsewhere. Perhaps even more strongly there than in most, for Sweden had long been oriented to the south, particularly to Germany, and Swedish critics had had little or no occasion to read American books. Their previous reading in American literature had produced, it is true, a few moments of enthusiasm—as when Fredrika Bremer published in mid-century her accounts of travels in American literary circles, and when Strindberg made his discovery of Mark Twain and other American humorists—but it had been otherwise little better than desultory. Indeed, for several decades most critics had been, at best, indifferent to America and American literature and regarded the very concept of an American literature as wholly indefensible. It was in this spirit of indifference, skepticism, and even hostility that they turned after the war to a more vigorous reading of American books than they had previously allowed themselves.

It is true, of course, that colonial and revolutionary America had once been the object of considerable Swedish interest and had then fared well with her critics, who for the most part shared the fairly universal admiration in Europe of the republic emerging across the Atlantic. This earlier, more generous Swedish view of America had had its beginnings in the colonization along the Delaware and in Swedish curiosity in a primeval, unspoiled land. But it had been mainly formulated when Washington and Franklin were being much admired for their part in establishing the success of a great experiment in political philosophy.[1] American literature was

---

[1] This and other information in this paragraph concerning the Swedish reaction to her American colonies and later to the Revolution and its aftermath, is taken from Harald Elovson, *Amerika i svensk litteratur, 1750–1820: En studie i komparativ litteraturhistoria,* Lund, 1930.

then translated into Swedish for the first time, when a poem by Freneau appeared in a prose version in *Stockholms-Posten* in 1779. *Poor Richard* was frequently translated in the following years, and all during the period American political documents found their way into the Swedish press. Swedish admiration of America as a political, economic, and religious refuge continued to grow, and in the early nineteenth century, during the general European dismay over the "imminent" downfall of Western civilization, America had often been looked upon as the hope of the future cultural life of man. The deep penetration of this attitude, which remained a stereotype in Swedish thinking for many years, is illustrated by a quotation from a Swedish textbook in world history published in 1821:

> This happy nation, where men rightly feel themselves to be men, increases in size with nearly every year. It is a haven for all of those who feel themselves sore oppressed by the unjust measures of their European masters; and if mercantilism there does not crowd out more noble occupations, if art and science may enjoy a more favorable protection, then it may well be in the future the site of the culture and happiness now fleeing from Europe.[2]

Signs of the later bitter distrust of American mercantilism are visible even here, but they were obviously discounted or ignored by the thousands of Swedish emigrants who turned this commonplace attitude toward America into a principle of action. In the succeeding decades they drained off about one-fifth of Sweden's population in their search for a new life or a new start in the old. In the meantime, American literature was being represented in Sweden chiefly by Cooper and Irving,[3] in spite of the moderately successful efforts of Fredrika Bremer to stimulate interest in a variety of American authors. Whatever cultural shortcomings America was said to have were usually generously excused by virtue of the promise, seemingly inherent in the new democracy, of better things to come.

All this, however, was soon to change. Toward the end of the nineteenth century, a strong distaste for America began to flourish among Swedish intellectuals. It soon so thoroughly displaced their earlier esteem that the idealistic view of America, though still held by some hopeful emigrants, had assumed, by World War I, clearly ironic overtones for the intellectuals at home. Some of their own number, upon returning from visits or attempts

---

[2] Quoted *ibid.*, p. 295, from Thomaeus' *Allmänna Werlds-Historien uti korrt samman-drag för den spädare ungdomen*, pp. 203—204.

[3] Ruben Berg, "Nordamerikansk litteratur i Sverige," in *Moderna Amerikaner*, Stockholm, 1925, pp. 149—186.

to settle in America, were telling a tale of life in America markedly different from the older, conventional story of democratic freedom and golden opportunity. America was for them no longer a haven, but a menace; it had become not a cause of hope, but of fear. The thousands of personal ties set up with America through the process of emigration did nothing to dull the asperity of this new criticism: for one thing, emigration had not yet become a public question worthy of careful official study, so that little was accurately known about it; for another, the privations and sufferings of many emigrants, though evidently not heavily publicized, were nevertheless known, so that if anything, their experience did more to strengthen than to weaken the new animus against America.

This, then, was the prevailing attitude toward America in which Swedish critics and ordinary Swedish readers began to read her literature after World War I. Since it determined the line taken in their criticism for many years, it is worth examining in some detail before we turn to specific criticism of American literature in the 1920's, the period we are principally interested in. As elusive of definition as "attitudes" can be, we must at least apprise ourselves of the important basic assumptions held by the Swedes about American culture and American literature in those years. Curiously enough, these assumptions not only constituted the starting point for much Swedish critical discussion of contemporary American literature, but they were ultimately responsible for the award in 1930 of the Nobel Prize for the first time to an American writer.

Fortunately, when we turn to essays and reviews on American literature appearing in Swedish journals and newspapers between 1910 and 1920 and later, the difficulties of our inquiry rapidly diminish, for a common strain in the Swedish approach toward American literature soon becomes apparent. Moreover, it is just as soon seen to be nothing essentially new to students of foreign reaction to America, for it incorporates attitudes with which we are already familiar in the British criticism of America current in no less remote a period than 1825 to 1845. It is a period which has been called one of "Tory condescension" in the history of British criticism of America.[4] Best known to us in the writings of the Rev. Isaac Fidler and of Mrs. Trollope, this sort of criticism is rarely favorable, and then only with labored condescension. Although it can be sprightly and amusing, it is more often shocked, indignant, or scornful as it recounts the peculiarly American sins of materialism, hypocrisy, and smugness. In

[4] For a summary with examples of this criticism, see Allan Nevins, *American Social History as Recorded by British Travellers*, New York, 1923, part II.

England it was soon superseded by something more objective and temperate, but occasionally it flared up again, as it did in the 1880's in the writings of Sir Lepel Griffin. In a representative passage which is also of particular interest to us, this critic of America wrote:

> America is the country of disillusion and disappointment, in politics, literature, culture, and art; in its scenery, its cities, and its people. With some experience of every country in the civilized world, I can think of none except Russia in which I would not prefer to reside, in which life would not be more worth living, less sordid and mean and unlovely.[5]

This passage, typical of its kind and, incidentally, suggesting the Scylla-and-Charybdis choice between America and Russia that was in a few decades to become a recurrent theme in Sweden, was one of many enthusiastically quoted[6] five years later by Knut Hamsun, the Norwegian novelist and winner of the Nobel Prize for literature in 1920. Published in Copenhagen in 1889 from lectures given there the previous winter and in Minneapolis in the spring of 1886,[7] *Fra det moderne Amerikas Aandsliv* ("The Cultural Life of Modern America") stems from Hamsun's two attempts to settle in Norwegian communities in midwestern America in 1882–1884 and 1886–1888. Although written by a Norwegian for a Dano-Norwegian audience, it of course made its way to Sweden and for four decades was regarded there as a source-book of discerning, "on-the-spot" criticism of America by one of Scandinavia's most distinguished authors. Moreover, the attitudes expressed in his book were echoed again and again in Swedish essays and articles on America and American books in the 'twenties and even in the 'thirties; so much was it in the air that reference could readily be made in reviews to it or to similar views expressed by Swedish writers who also had experienced personal disappointment in America.

Hamsun's book has the rhetorical stamp of lectures delivered by a forceful man highly conscious of his audience and not unwilling to win their assent by reciting striking "statistics" and by interlarding his pages of scornful criticism with whimsy, exaggeration, mock horror, and heavy-handed irony.[8] The voice and figure of Kurt Hamsun are ineradically

---

[5] Sir Lepel Griffin, "A Visit to Philistia," *Fortnightly Review,* XLI, n.s. XXXV (January 1884), 50.

[6] Knut Hamsun, *Fra det moderne Amerikas Aandsliv,* Copenhagen, 1889, p. 249.

[7] Einar Skavlan, *Knut Hamsun,* Oslo, 1929, p. 125.

[8] Einar Skavlan, *op. cit.,* p. 151, attributes these qualities to a strain of humor in the manner of Mark Twain, and indeed of all American authors Hamsun most admired

present when one reads *Fra det moderne Amerikas Aandsliv,* and the book is as typical of the rebellious, energetic author as it is of a kind of criticism soon thereafter in the ascendant in Sweden. Yet for all its personal qualities, it is not only the prototype of what Swedish writers were to say about America, but it was long remembered for itself as a compendium of truths about America. Thus, for example, Hamsun's book was referred to as late as 1929 by a Swedish reviewer of Harold Stearns's compilation, *Civilization in the United States.* According to the reviewer, the novelist Hjalmar Söderberg publicly thanked Hamsun for his book on America because it had removed from his own mind any idea of going to the New World.[9] In 1932 a critic of a Swedish book on America which we shall later examine, called it "perhaps the best that has been written about the U.S.A. in a Scandinavian language since Knut Hamsun's *Fra det moderne Amerikas Aandsliv.*"[10]

Nothing pleased Hamsun, just as nothing had pleased Sir Lepel Griffin. After an opening section in which Hamsun deplored American chauvinism, American preoccupation with money, American waste, and American intellectual smugness, he devoted the major part of his book to a critique

Twain and perhaps intended to imitate him in the lighter moments of his lectures. But as Skavlan agrees, the book's chief purpose was a serious attack on America and especially on the American concept of freedom, whose praise by Björnstjerne Björnson, a boyhood hero of Hamsun's who had lately lost some standing in his admirer's eyes, rankled Hamsun. In his preface to *Hunger* (New York, 1920) Edwin Björkman reprints (p. vii) an inscription by Hamsun on the flyleaf of his copy of *Fra det moderne Amerikas Aandsliv:* "A youthful work. It has ceased to represent my opinion of America." Skavlan also reports (p. 152) that Hamsun later modified his opinions of America and would not permit the book to be reprinted, yet "he insists that the book in all its essentials was accurate." Skavlan himself says of the book (p. 146): *"Fra det moderne Amerikas Aandsliv* is a sprightly, entertaining book—excellently written, astonishing in its language, which is as tight-fitting as a silk dress over its bold contents. It is one of the most important books in Norwegian literature. Forty years old, it is timely even now—and seems new and fresh when read today. It may well be that many things in this attack on American culture were pushed too hard by the young, disrespectful Hamsun. But time has pushed even harder in the forty years since then; America has gone on to push itself over the whole world. And that 'culture' that the young Hamsun scourged in his book we recognize all about us in many things which had not revealed themselves so clearly in Norway at that time. The book is even better today than when it was written."

[9] Hälge Emilson, "Amerikansk kulturkritik," *SDS,* August 18, 1929. (For abbreviations of newspaper sources cited, see List of Abbreviations Used, p. 13.) The review also recalls Söderberg's witticism, which delighted generations of Swedes, that he would gladly travel to America if he did not have to go ashore.

[10] Artur Möller, "Gustaf Hellström," *Ord och Bild,* XLI (1932), 453.

of American literature. Since this section is the heart of the book and is typical of the whole, and since it concerns a subject of particular interest to us, we may examine it profitably in some detail.

Because Americans are too much occupied with making money, Hamsun wrote, they are not interested in art. "Literature has no force in American life. . . . People do not read to become more fully developed, but . . . to be thrilled by the bloody scenes in detective stories, moved to tears by the . . . novels of Charlotte Braeme, and put to rest in the evenings by the great, sleepy Longfellow,"[11] although there are, he admitted, a few exceptions. Newspapers in America are the greatest source of reading matter, but they are devoted mainly to reporting robberies, murder, scandal, births, deaths, and marriages. American literature, he continued,

> is hopelessly unreal and devoid of talent. It has in it love and gun-shooting, but it does not have the pulse of life beating in it; it is without life's red richness; it lacks emotion. I make exception, of course, of a few authors whose books a modern man can endure to read; I except Mark Twain, that pale pessimist who with his wonderful wit and humor is without antecedent or successor in America;[12] I except a little of Poe, a little of Hawthorne, a little of Harte. But in the long run American literature is not the expression of American life, as are the newspapers. It makes no impression, it is not earthy enough, it chatters too much and feels too little; it has too much poetizing and too little reality; it does not depict, it chants, speaks with eyes turned toward heaven, occupies itself with virtue and Boston morality, preaches, exhorts, puts morocco bindings around unswerving loyalty and a heroic Indian couple.[13]

As with other things in America, literature lags far behind current developments in Europe, Hamsun declared. Americans have not gone beyond Dickens and Scott in the novel and Milton and Longfellow in poetry, so that, he complained, it is impossible to find a trace of modernity in American literature. The bookshops handle only "respectable" books, and in the single bookshop in Minneapolis, a city the size of Copenhagen, Hamsun could find only

[11] Knut Hamsun, *op. cit.*, p. 36.

[12] Hamsun could assume that Twain and the other writers he mentioned were known to his audience, all having by 1889 found their way into translation in Scandinavia; one of Twain's translators, incidentally, was August Strindberg, whose *Amerikanska humorister* (Stockholm, 1878) had also included sketches by Artemus Ward, Charles Dudley Warner, and others.

[13] Knut Hamsun, *op. cit.*, pp. 52—53.

decorated greeting cards, verse collections in gold jackets, detective stories, sheet music for *Yankee Doodle* and *Home Sweet Home,* blessed Longfellow, and all possible variations of the most successful ink-stands. It also contains a flood of American fiction made possible by a large population of female scribblers. And the bookstore is of course a patriotic one; it has the history of the wars of the U.S. and lithographs of Washington; it has "Uncle Tom's Cabin" and General Grant's memoirs.[14]

What he found in the bookstore was largely duplicated in the town library, which, he reported, had all the books produced by Americans, all of Scott's and Dickens's novels, all those by Dumas *père,* Sue, Verne, Marryat and Pellico, but not one by Zola, Bourget, the Goncourts, the Russians, the Scandinavians (except for Andersen's tales)—and ask for Hartmann, Comte, Schopenhauer, and the librarian will pointedly remark that "of philosophers he has Emerson."[15]

Hamsun then concentrated his criticism on Twain, Whitman, and Emerson. Although Twain, he felt, cannot be called truly creative *(en Digter),* "he makes people smile while he himself sits weeping; he is a pessimist, humorist, and satirist."[16] Whitman, on the other hand, had in Hamsun's view few saving qualities; *Leaves of Grass* is no more a song than is a multiplication table. It is in "pure prose form, without any meter or rhyme whatever," and Whitman is a wild man, "a voice of Nature in an uncultivated primordial land" *(en Naturlyd i et urdyrket Urland).*[17] His diction is Indian and Old Testament in long catalogs of words that pour out spontaneously without meaning; it is impossible to say what he intends: "In the art of talking much and saying absolutely nothing, I have never met his equal."[18] To follow Whitman's biographers' suggestion that one study his life in order to understand his poetry is useless, for so little occurred in his life:

> If he had been born in a civilized country and intelligently reared, he could perhaps have become a little Wagner; his nerves are sensitive and his temperament musical; but born in America, that backwoods [*Afegn*] of the world, where everything shouts hurrah and whose people's sole acknowledged talent

[14] *Ibid.,* p. 55.
[15] *Ibid.,* p. 59.
[16] *Ibid.,* p. 63.
[17] *Ibid.,* p. 64. An English translation of the entire section on Whitman is available in Gay W. Allen, *Walt Whitman Abroad,* Syracuse, 1955, pp. 112–123.
[18] *Ibid.,* p. 72.

is for making money, he might have become a transitional figure, something between a primitive nature and a modern man.[19]

Hamsun concluded that Whitman, though fundamentally a good man, warm-hearted and lovable, is enormously, monstrously naive. "His mind is too restless and his thoughts are too undisciplined to settle on the simple things he sees and to sing about them; he depicts life in parade, not the fine subtleties of a particular thing, but the noisy diversity of all things; he always sees masses."[20] Hamsun thought the "Calamus" poems best with their theme of love for one's fellow—at least, he added, they are readable. But on the whole, Whitman "is rather a richer personality than he is a talented poet. For Walt Whitman cannot write. But he can feel. He lives a life of feeling. If he had not received that letter from Emerson, his book would have fallen noiselessly to the ground—which it deserved."[21]

Emerson in his turn had little to please Hamsun, for although it was admitted that Emerson has fine powers of observation and writes "tasteful things, interesting things, good things," his criticism is haphazard when it should be modern, scientific. "He is the last little critic of the tyranny of rules. As Shakespeare is his highest rule in the drama, Plato is his highest rule in philosophy,"[22] and his thinking is limited by Christian principles: "Just as he is a moralist in his criticism, so is he a Unitarian in his philosophy."[23]

In concluding the section on American literature, Hamsun fixed the necessary condition for the redemption of American culture:

Whitman and Emerson have been presented as the particularly national representatives of their country's literature—not to the unconditional advantage of America: the one is an inarticulate poet and the other a literary sermonizer. I am not for a moment in doubt that America's literature needs the influence of foreign and further advanced literatures, which Congress now patriotically puts a duty upon. If it is to become a means of development, it must change in both form and content. But first there must arise *doubters* in that great land, men and women who doubt that America is culturally the richest country in the world. National smugness must be undermined, patriotism must get a setback.[24]

[19] *Ibid.*, p. 76.
[20] *Ibid.*, p. 79.
[21] *Ibid.*, p. 85.
[22] *Ibid.*, p. 90.
[23] *Ibid.*, p. 114.
[24] *Ibid.*, pp. 129—130.

We may anticipate a later chapter by saying here that in the Swedish view this condition was partially fulfilled by American literature of the 1920's, and that Sinclair Lewis came to fill the role of the "doubter" that Hamsun had demanded.

After reviewing in similarly high-handed fashion American drama and debunking the traditional concept of America as the land of freedom, Hamsun, ever a believer in the efficacy of the hero in shaping the destiny of mankind, brought his book to a close in a minor key; he disavowed any hope that there might arise in a nation made up of simple folk, "bankrupts and criminals, adventurers and the insane, preachers and Negroes," one noble soul or "one seeker of light, one spirit in rebellion, who could deviate, set the tempo, step out with the first intentional misstep"; for in America "all plod through life harmoniously accompanied by high hurrahs, without looking around even once." America belongs to "a world of bawling and steam and great, noisy, stamping machines," and is "a nation of that world with people of all areas, from the Nordic whites to the tropic's apes and intellectual mulattoes."[25]

Despite the labored superciliousness of much of this criticism, its meaning was unmistakable and its intemperance probably seemed appropriate to a courageous, ruthless revelation—at last—of the "truth about America." Less biased and less vehement criticism could not have looked for the sensational, lasting effect that Hamsun's book produced. Not only was it remembered for itself, but the attitudes contained in it were confirmed many times over, sometimes in direct criticism, but more often indirectly in novels, plays, and poetry. These later animadversions—at least in Sweden, where our present interest wholly lies—were seldom as vituperative as Hamsun's had been, but they were clearly of the same sort, as a few of the more noteworthy instances will show.

Of the Swedish writers who continued Hamsun's line of attack in their criticism of American culture, the three most significant to our inquiry are Per Hallström, Henning Berger, and Gustaf Hellström. Both Hallström and Hellström were to be elected—in 1908 and 1942 respectively—to membership in "The Eighteen" of the Swedish Academy, Hallström's election coming early enough to give him a vote in the three-man committee that awarded the Nobel Prize to Sinclair Lewis in 1930. Hallström came to America some ten years after Hamsun. Trained as an engineer, he spent most of his time in America in a Philadelphia factory. Like Hamsun, he

---

[25] *Ibid.*, pp. 253—255.

returned home after a few short years, bitter and disappointed, and in his early volume of short stories, *Vilsna fåglar* (1894), he spilled out his revulsion for America and the death that he felt it signifies for the "inner life." The tone of the stories is one of dreariness and despair in the face of the deadening competition inherent in the struggle for existence in a raw, uncultured, industrialized society. It is clear that America became for Hallström a symbol of metropolitan, mechanized life that destroys individualism and the life of the imagination. In 1913 the influential critic Professor Fredrik Böök published a detailed analysis of the stories which serves to indicate for us both the background of the stories and the importance attached to them in Sweden. Böök associated Hallström's bitterness and melancholy directly with the rebirth of Schopenhauerism in the 'nineties, but Hallström's unhappiness in his choice of a career and the loneliness and uncertainties of his young manhood added sensibly to his pessimism and his profound discontent with both himself and the times. Böök quotes Hallström's own comments on these two or three years as he published them in 1902 ("En sparf i tranedans"): "Nor did anyone have a thinner skin than I to withstand hardships. My work did not suit me, and it was a hard trial to seem one thing and to be another ... My outlook on life was dark to an extreme."[26] Without a public yet for his poetry to give him the support which he desperately needed, he took ship for America, "which seems," Hallström confessed,

> to have been about the most stupid thing I could have done. If practical life oppressed me here, what should it not do over there in its so much harsher and sterner forms! I went without illusions, with no intention of remaining, only with the need of seeing something of the world, of running right into the arms of the monster Utility instead of being teased by its tail. ... [However, in America] the spirit of optimistic materialism became no more attractive by clothing itself as Christian. Dogmatism in looking on life ... seemed to me only narrowminded. The grinning crudities of advertising and politics aroused in me only opposition. In addition, there was the contempt of a colossal factory system for human life.[27]

In this frame of mind, Böök says, Hallström wrote *Vilsna fåglar,* and thus, for example, one can understand Doctor Braun in the first sketch in the book as a spokesman for Hallström: "He is doomed [Böök concludes] to

[26] Cited in Fredrik Böök, "Hallströms tidigare novellistik," in *Svenska studier i litteraturvetenskap,* Stockholm, 1913, p. 251.

[27] *Ibid.,* pp. 252—253.

witness, powerless, the triumph of egoism and intellectual vacuity, 'to see mediocrity grow fatter and stupidity more stupid.' He belongs to the embittered opposition which has thrust aside 'the corrupted name of idealism.' Gray weather over the streets of Philadelphia is the very gloom of the times."[28]

Hallström repeated his views of America in a newspaper interview in 1928, when he declared that there were American writers of the day to be taken seriously, for in their social criticism, he said, they were attacking the greatest defect in the American character: smugness. Another serious defect Hallström declared to be American optimism. Although it allows Americans to go about their business cheerfully, it tends nevertheless to make them think and act superficially. The Americans' chief virtue is their good humor, a result of their southerly climate and therefore absurd for Swedes to try to imitate, for "what we are Americanized in is American superficiality; in a word, we would become a kind of second-class American, which we must with all our might seek to prevent. . . . [American influence in Europe] is the unfortunate consequence of the war. . . . I saw that danger early during the war and predicted that it would come."[29]

Though of lesser stature than Hallström, another writer with similar American experiences, Henning Berger, produced short stories and novels taking in effect Hamsun's view of America. His impressions of Chicago in the 'nineties were gathered up in his first book, *Där ute* (Stockholm, 1901), upon his return to Sweden. As thin and crudely fashioned as much of Berger's writing is, Fredrik Böök, editor in 1927 of a reprinting of Berger's first volume, nevertheless called this collection of stories about Swedish immigrants in America one of Berger's best:

> [*Där ute*] reproduces his own memories of the eight years he spent in the U.S. In his later writing he has often dilated and romanticized the impressions he received in America and the incidents he experienced there; in *Där ute* he presents them more faithfully and more simply. . . . With a clear eye he has captured the scenes of the big city and the landscape of the streets; and he had the art of evoking all the changing pictures on the retina somewhat as

[28] *Ibid.*, p. 259.
[29] "P. J. E.," "Amerikansk Självgodhet, Parlamentariskt Tragglande och Fascistiskt Tyranni hota den samtida kulturvärlden; En Intervju med Per Hallström," *NDA,* January 15, 1928. In a volume of short stories, *Händelser,* Stockholm, 1927, Hallström included as his first three stories ("George," "Doktor Blood," "Den främmande") anecdotes from his days in Philadelphia, all of which bore out his earlier condemnation of the ruthlessness and ugliness of American materialism.

a photographer develops his plates. It is not a profound art, but when it has to do with the fate of the Swedish emigrants this limitation has little significance, for what is characteristic of their existence in the New World is precisely that it is taken up in the outer sensations, that it is sucked in in the mighty maelstrom of the material life.[30]

The first of the stories tells of that rare bird, the immigrant who became wealthy, but at the expense, Berger wishes us to know, of his self-respect and a sense of belonging: the old country, once denied, is forever lost to him, and the new offers no place for roots to sink in. In contrast, the second story tells of the immigrant who became not only spiritually but physically lost as well, for young Emil, hopeful and sanguine about his prospects in America in his early letters to "dear mamma" home in Sweden, meets with bad luck from the beginning; four years later, when Emil's whereabouts have become unknown, his former landlord replies to the desperate mother's plea for information about her son that although Emil had been a likely-looking lad, he like so many other immigrants, could find no employment, was soon too drunk even to hold a job, and finally disappeared. Other stories tell how an obscure, faithful Swedish bookkeeper after a lifetime of meticulous service is summarily fired by his new American boss in the interest, ostensibly, of "efficiency"; how another immigrant finally dies of a heart attack after trying to live a hurried, Americanized life in an unscrupulous pursuit of dollars; how an artist forced in America to turn street peddler has a stroke of luck and "for a moment forgot that he was in the land of egotism in the era of ruthlessness"; and so on. The total picture presented in *Där ute* is grim without relief: America destroys either life or soul—or both. The principal themes of the stories, American conceit, American vulgarity, and American inhumanity, are viewed in the same light as that in which Hamsun had seen them.[31]

The most vehement Swedish criticism of America and the closest to Hamsun's in spirit if not in details, came from Henning Berger's comrade, Gustaf Hellström, who augmented his income from literary efforts by reporting for a Stockholm daily on the international scene from London, Paris, and finally, from 1918 to 1921, New York. Predisposed to take a

[30] Fredrik Böök, "Inledning," in Henning Berger, *Där ute*, Stockholm, 1927, pp. [3—4].
[31] Henning Berger used American settings and themes in later novels and stories, the most ambitious of them being *Hägringen, Bendel & Co,* and *Fata morgana,* a trilogy on wheat speculation given in 1922 the collective title *Drömlandet.*

positive view of American life by his admiration of President Wilson, by his marriage to an American painter, and by his eagerness to get away from war-weary Paris to fresh surroundings, he was determined to avoid the tourist's hasty, superficial judgments. For his first volume on the United States, *Förenta staterna och världsfreden* (Stockholm, 1919), chiefly an explanation of Wilson's position as President, his background, and his relationship with the political parties, Hellström assembled a small but impressive bibliography that included Bryce's *Commonwealth,* Wilson's *History of the American People,* books by A. M. Simons, S. D. Fess, John Fiske, and a few French and German commentaries. In his opening chapter Hellström analyzed the American character and began by saying that only a few months' visit in America is needed to realize that current European opinion of America is "not only superficial and incorrect, but at bottom a sham," for everything fundamental to American life is minimized in the formulation of that opinion and everything merely incidental or unique is subjected to microscopic inspection. The difficulty, Hellström explained, lies in the fact that Europeans have allowed their judgment of America to be formed by newspaper accounts of the "vulgar" American taste, "dollar-princesses," the lack of literature and art, materialism, and Tammany politics. Such a judgment, he declared, is based on European snobbishness and on the disappointed hopes of those who have failed in the New World, not on the facts. And in this first book, Hellström tells his readers of the "facts" of the personal cleanliness of the Americans, their vitality, good humor, and straightforward, honest friendliness. He speaks of the salutary effects of Puritanism, which though originally quite severe, has been softened into a more humane religiosity; he speaks of the splendid American libraries with their excellent selection of books; he speaks, in short, in warm praise of everything he felt to be significant in American life. But in one year's time all this was changed. Abandoning bibliographies and giving vent to his own feelings, Hellström published a second book on America, this time a two-volume novel called *Ett rekommendationsbrev* (Stockholm, 1920). It is disappointing as a novel, as all critics have agreed, but its castigation of America in the spirit of Hamsun was well received as astute criticism.

Random quotations from the novel will suffice to identify that criticism, for characterization is unimportant and the disjointed narrative was merely a hook on which Hellström could hang his revised opinions of America. The narrator in the novel, a newcomer to America, is warned in advance by an American expatriate to leave no doubt in the minds of his hosts that he believes America to be "the number one country" of the world; he is told that "in its proper meaning, there is no such thing as conversation in American social life," and that for the sake of his social standing he should be careful in speaking with women because of their "social superiority over man in America." The key to the mystery of the American character lies in the term "joker": "There is, of course, bluff in America, much bluff. But there is something else: the joker! Draw no conclusions until the game is over. You never know how an American may act. The joker will suddenly appear in the deal and the value of the cards has been changed."[32] Skyscrapers, those arrogant violations of all that is natural, evoke a dark brown mood in the hero, and riding in an automobile in dense traffic stirs him to muse on the meaning of life in America: "All these people who hurried past in their rolling, flower-bedecked boudoirs reflected in their facial expression the self-reliance and assured consciousness of having mastered the two greatest obstacles to human progress: credit and distance."[33] Hellström singles out for closer examination a few of these self-assured people and in the process arrives at some rather sensational generalizations about American dishonesty, brutality, sexual frigidity in women, smugness, and cultural aridity. Whole sections of the book deal gratuitously and caustically with the plight of the Negro in America, the hypocrisy of a kept press, the badgering of unions by capitalists, and the exploitation of immigrant labor. American literature, according to various persons sympathetically portrayed by Hellström, is far removed from reality; the poetry has "strangely and symbolically enough been drawn from Chinese miniature poetry. The gap between reality and this poetry can hardly be imagined greater. The novel in its turn draws nine-tenths of its motives from an existence which to living Americans is close to being foreign: Wild West romanticism."[34] Lyric poetry suffers from a lack of a

---

[32] Gustaf Hellström, *Ett rekommendationsbrev*, Stockholm, 1920, p. 28. Cf. the following passage from Hellström's first book on America (*Förenta staterna och världsfreden*, p. 35): "For he who believes that America's enormous economic upswing has its roots principally in financial recklessness, in the unscrupulous trampling underfoot of the rights of others, commits a disastrous mistake when it comes to a proper evaluation of the Americans. There is very little bluff in America, even in American poker."

[33] *Ett rekommendationsbrev*, p. 111.

[34] *Ibid.*, p. 257. Five years after writing this, Hellström used the term "Wild West" in another sense in attempting to show how much modern American literature has depended upon the work of "western" writers like Hamlin Garland, Frank Norris, and Theodore Dreiser. His long essay, "'Vilda Västern' i nyare amerikansk litteratur," *Vår Tid*, X (1925), 47—91, is unique in Swedish criticism of the period in carefully working out a

strong native folk tradition in poetry, and its ties with European traditions have been weakened by adherence to the standards of a middle class of a particularly despicable kind, the consciously ignorant and self-sufficient middle class. And finally, American literature is so bad because it is written by the very worst crowd—which makes it genuinely democratic, as one of the characters says, but which also results in its animosity toward ideas, its conventionality, its total lack of truthfulness, and its insufferable moralizing.[35] In other words, the complaint here is that there is, to use Knut Hamsun's term, no cultural elite in America, an observation already made by Hamsun and implied by Per Hallström and Henning Berger.

Of more than passing interest to us in Hellström's novel is the character Ruskin Howard, around whom much of the action takes place. His tailored and barbered appearance, his sharp nasal tones, his indeterminate age, his "healthy, hygienic pallor," his dry complexion of someone who has lived long in a tropical climate without sun ("a kind of electrically lighted tropic"), and the friendly distance, like that of royalty, which he maintains —these "typical" attributes of the American businessman lead Hellström to speculate ominously on their peculiarity and on the possibility latent in them of the development of a "new white race: the American." Ruskin Howard shows himself in the novel to be a ruthless, high-handed financier empty of almost every human sentiment; he is strongly reminiscent of the stereotyped caricature of the Wall Street capitalist portrayed as grandly careless of human values in his unscrupulous machinations for wealth and power. Because of the great difference between Hellström's expository method of characterization and tendency toward caricature on the one hand, and Sinclair Lewis's ironic dramatization of character through action and a wealth and intimacy of subsidiary detail on the other, it is only partly true that, as a Swedish critic has pointed out,[36] in Hellström's novel are the makings of a Babbitt or a Dodsworth; Ruskin Howard is too much a mere target for Hellström's abuse to permit more than a superficial comparison with Lewis's characters. Yet the very fact that such a comparison

---

plausible historical and social background of the literature; in tone and method it has none of the rancor or vast generalizations of his novel and may be said, therefore, to be one more bit of evidence of the change in Swedish criticism of America that took place in the 'twenties, as it will be described in a later chapter.

[35] *Ibid.*, pp. 259—261.

[36] Holger Ahlenius, *Gustaf Hellström*, Stockholm, 1934 (Studentföreningen Verdandis småskrifter no. 364), p. 28. The observation is repeated without reservation in Henrik Schück and Karl Warburg, *Svensk litteraturhistoria*, VIII (by Erik Hj. Linder), Stockholm, 1949 (hereafter cited as Schück–Warburg VIII), p. 78.

has been made is suggestive of the expectations of "authentic" American subject matter that were engendered in the minds of the Swedish public by Hellström and others. What that public expected they were to find in Sinclair Lewis and the writers that were grouped with him, such as Edith Wharton, whose Pauline Manford in *Twilight Sleep* the same critic might well have said to have been foreshadowed by Alice Smith in Hellström's novel.

That the criticism of American life embodied in Hellström's *Ett rekommendationsbrev* became established as one more expression of the Swedish attitude toward America is amply attested. We have already quoted the critic[37] who called it "perhaps the best that has been written about the U.S.A. in a Scandinavian language since Knut Hamsun's *Fra det moderne Amerikas Aandsliv.*" Another, the chief librarian of the Royal Library in Stockholm, wrote of Hellström's novel that "above all, the author has succeeded brilliantly in catching a significant characteristic of the American character, namely, the nervous eagerness to have something to do, to organize some charitable work, to set in motion some reform or to pursue some similar movement in the collective interest of the recognized American."[38] In the authoritative history of modern Swedish literature Erik Hj. Linder writes of *Ett rekommendationsbrev* that it is

> a typical novel of reporting ... [but] the book can be read today for its many-sided and convincing depiction of America.... The special position of women, the aftereffects of Puritanism in public morals, the frustrated sexuality, the indulgence in spectacular, business-like charity, the relation between advertised acts of charity and one's social career, doctrinaire capitalism united with a good portion of intelligent cynicism, the weak labor organizations, the dependence of the press on its powerful owners, the Negro problem in the South —all this passes in review and is introduced in an ingeniously composed, sometimes exciting sequence of events....
>
> As a novel of reporting the book is brilliant and biting; as a human and artistic document it displays certain shortcomings.... But one forgets these deficiencies for the factual sharpness and the good humor.[39]

Even more telling evidence of the hold such views as Hellström's and his predecessors' had on the Swedish mind is to be found in the frequent references to them in the reviews and criticism of the time. Sometimes the

[37] *Supra,* p. 19.
[38] Oscar Wieselgren, "Gustaf Hellström," *Biblioteksbladet,* XVI (1932), 10.
[39] Schück—Warburg, VIII, p. 78.

reference is specific, in lines like these from a review in 1929 of a novel by Edith Wharton:

Ten years ago Gustaf Hellström characterized an American in these penetrating words: He does not think, he only plans. The most fundamental characteristics of a Mr. Babbitt could not be expressed more precisely or concisely....[40]

Much more often, of course, no specific reference of this sort was made, yet the critic's point of view was unmistakably familiar. In the development of his critical remarks on a newly translated American book, he would simply take for granted that he and his readers were *en rapport* in their attitudes toward America. We may best illustrate the adoption of this critical tone when we shall have before us, in later chapters, lengthy quotations of reviews and criticism of certain American authors whose reception in Sweden is to be examined in some detail.

In all the forty years from 1890 to 1930 not one important voice in Swedish literature was raised in dissent from these views, which were also worked into the writings of lesser authors. The popular novels of Hilma Angered-Strandberg lent support to the concept of America as a country without tradition and preoccupied with money-making: *Den nya världen* (Stockholm, 1898) told of the failure in America of two Swedish immigrants, one dying of a heat stroke after tramping the streets of Chicago in a vain search for work, the other, his wife, coming close to prostitution in order to survive, and finally committing suicide; *På prärien* (Stockholm, 1898) told of the cultivated Matilda Hjelm's experience in coming to the prairie town of Morton as the new wife of a "professor" at a Swedish Lutheran college—her story being not unlike Carol Kennicott's in *Main Street* in revealing the narrowness of intellectual life and the dearth of real conversation in a small pioneer town. A few years later, K. G. Ossiannilsson's series of sketches and anecdotes about life in America[41] gave Swedish readers lightly ironic glimpses of American customs and manners in such diverse activities as courting, politics, religion, business, the treatment of immigrants, and so on. Although certainly not intended to constitute a serious indictment of American life, the stories made their point consistently in the bemused bewilderment and shock of an urbane European in a land of unconcealed double-dealing and crassness. At the same time, the poetaster Sigurd Agrell, dispensing entirely with Ossiannilsson's urbanity and in fact

[40] A[nnie] L[öfste]dt, "Mrs. Manford från U. S. A.," *GHT*, November 29, 1929; reprinted under the same title in the author's *En kvinna om böcker*, Stockholm, 1932, pp. 103–107.
[41] K. G. Ossiannilsson, *Amerikaner och Byzantiner*, Stockholm, 1905.

discomfited by it, expressed the view of his little coterie of writers in a broadside blast in verse which included the lines:

> You we call Americans,
> You men with two inches of hide,
> Who live off pork and chicanery
> And pray to the dollar and God![42]

And much later, when the major playwright and novelist Hjalmar Bergman returned from three months in Hollywood in 1923, he could produce a farce like *Dollar* (Stockholm, 1926), which played upon popular concepts about American *nouveaux riches* and their naive view of culture, though not, as before, so much for didactic or self-expressive reasons as for the entertainment value inherent in the easy ridicule of America through these concepts.

From Per Hallström to Gustaf Hellström and Hjalmar Bergman, therefore, no Swedish writer of consequence in four decades altered in any essential the concept of American life ventilated by Knut Hamsun in Copenhagen in 1889. America was still conceived of as a primitive land peopled with the dregs of European society and the jungles of Africa and excessively proud of its material advantages, a land where not only the life of the imagination and spirit is impossible but physical life precarious. Or as the poet Erik Axel Karlfeldt, chairman of the committee that awarded the Nobel Prize to Sinclair Lewis, put it in the final line of his poem "Ungdom," the dilemma of Swedish youth in modern times is that they are caught between two Gorgons: "i öster barbari, i väster miljardism"—literally, "to the east, barbarianism; to the west, billionairism."[43] Which is just about as far as Sir Lepel Griffin, "that amusing reversion to Mrs. Trollope," as he has been called, had got in 1884.

---

[42] Vi kalla er amerikaner,
ni män med två tums hud
som lefva af fläsk och chikaner
och bedja till dollarn och Gud!

—from Sigurd Agrell, " 'Decadenter' ..." in *Arabesker,* Stockholm, 1903, p. 58.

[43] Erik Axel Karlfeldt, "Ungdom," in *Hösthorn,* Stockholm, 1932, p. 124.

CHAPTER II

Swedish Criticism Before 1920: The Reception of Jack London and Upton Sinclair

It was not unnatural that Swedish critics should share the attitudes toward American culture which Swedish poets and novelists were expressing in their work. The opening sentence of a review in 1916 of Ernest Poole's *The Harbor* places before us in conveniently brief form the central position then being taken by every Swedish critic of American culture:

> It cannot be helped that we Europeans regard transatlantic culture with suspicion and prejudice, and that we have good grounds for considering America's literary and artistic achievements not only decidedly mediocre but even considerably inferior to what the Old World has produced.[1]

In support of this position, the reviewer adverted to a theory of the Americans' natural inferiority now quite familiar to us:

> In the great republic on the other side of the ocean, different peoples, nations, and races have been thrown together.... In this mixture a strange deposit has settled which is called American culture and which has raised so many different expectations and hopes for the future. Regardless of how many opinions there may be on the subject, a high national artistic culture can have little hope of thriving until the separate elements of the population ... have been fused into one new, stable entity. For us Europeans, who have an older culture, America has therefore become the land of mechanized civilization and of unlimited material possibilities, while at the same time it remains a country of extremely limited scientific and artistic possibilities.

Criticism of American culture was up against a stone wall; it could not advance, it could only repeat its prejudices. Of course, most critics chose rather to remain altogether silent on such an unfruitful subject, and as a result, reviews of American books from the period 1900 to 1920 are hard to come by. It was denied that an American literature existed, except

[1] Sven Rosén, "Modern amerikansk romankonst," *Stockholms Dagblad,* January 9, 1916.

perhaps as a sickly offshoot of English literature, and even though a few concessions could be made for individual American authors, these seemed crude, remote, primitive—or, most commonly, merely the authors of children's books.

Admittedly, however, the scattering of American literature then available in Swedish translation could have encouraged only the rash to read and write on books from a literature that was said to be virtually nonexistent. Among the American authors whose names appeared most frequently on Swedish publishing lists during the first two decades of the century were Louisa May Alcott, Frances Hodgson Burnett, James O. Curwood, and G. B. McCutcheon, all of them writing for young people and children. Bret Harte's *Gabriel Conroy* had been translated in 1876, but he was known exclusively as the author of books for children. Harriet Beecher Stowe's *Onkel Toms stuga* remained a perennial favorite, usually much abridged in a child's version as a sentimental tale of Eva, Topsy, and Uncle Tom. Edward Bellamy's *Looking Backward* seems to have attracted serious attention at the turn of the century, but the translations of books by such writers as Gertrude Atherton, Francis Marion Crawford, and Frank Stockton faded silently and quickly away from public notice. *The Scarlet Letter* had been translated into Swedish first in 1873 and again in 1916, and *The House of the Seven Gables* had appeared in Swedish in 1874, but Hawthorne was chiefly known as the author of tales for young people. The nineteenth-century impetus given by Fredrika Bremer to the reading of Emerson was still enough to bring an occasional volume on the market, but his reputation was as slight as that in Sweden of his representative mystic, Swedenborg. Henry James' *Roderick Hudson* had been translated in 1877 and *The American* in 1884; "Eugene Pickering" had appeared separately as *En filosofisk qvinna* in 1876, and collections of James' stories had been published in 1880 (*Fyra berättelser*) and 1893 (*Fru de Mauves . . .*). But in the Swedish view, James was decidedly an English author, and no marked interest was taken in him, moreover, until the 'forties—still as an Englishman.

The three best known American authors of the nineteenth century were Twain, Poe (both enjoying renewed interest at the close of World War I), and Cooper. Nearly thirty editions of Mark Twain's books (principally *Tom Sawyer* and *Huckleberry Finn*) appeared in translation between 1900 and 1920; but although he could be, as we have seen, a favorite of Knut Hamsun's and esteemed by Strindberg, his reputation in Sweden was as a writer of some unusually good books for youngsters.

Although Poe's stories went through some ten editions in varying combinations between 1900 and 1920, he seems to have been known chiefly as the author of such school pieces as "The Gold Bug" and "The Bells," the latter in a brilliant and popular translation by Viktor Rydberg. Even in later years, when the rise of interest in contemporary American literature served to revitalize the reputation of older authors, Poe, unlike Twain, seemed to make little appeal to the Swedish imagination. Cooper, on the other hand, was always popular. Twenty-three editions of his books were published between 1900 and 1920, and although he was never regarded as more than an author of adventure stories and romances, his was a name every Swedish reader was certain to know. "Communication between Swedish and American literature has not been especially lively," concluded the critic of *The Harbor*. "The most widely read of earlier American authors has probably been Cooper, whose name is known throughout the world and whom we remember as the author of the Indian books of our childhood."

Of the older authors, Twain, Poe, and Cooper were therefore the chief representatives of American literature in the years before 1920. Howells was virtually unknown, only his *A Foregone Conclusion* having been translated (1876). Melville's *Typee* had appeared in Swedish in 1879 as *Teipi*, and again in 1917 in a very much abridged form as an adventure-thriller for boys, this time called *I kannibalernas våld*, "In the Grip of the Cannibals." It was not until 1943, when *Moby-Dick* appeared, that there was enough active interest in Melville to support serious translation and publication in Swedish of his most important work. As for Southern writers, neither Simms, Cable, nor Glasgow had been translated. Frank Norris seems to have found a ready audience for his books, five appearing in translation between 1904 and 1918, including *The Pit, The Octopus,* and *Moran of the Lady Letty*. But these were published in cheap editions, sometimes at less than a crown a copy, not the kind of publication likely to come under review by a busy critic with no prior interest in American literature. Stephen Crane was entirely overlooked. Dreiser was not to appear in Swedish translation until 1927.

Two contemporary American authors, however, had amassed extraordinary numbers of readers, even though they may be said to have enjoyed no reputation whatever among serious readers and the major Swedish critics. Upton Sinclair and Jack London entered Sweden through the kitchen door and factory gate and seldom penetrated to the upstairs parlors and lecture halls of "respectable" literature, yet London set new bookselling records in Sweden, and Sinclair's readers, though many fewer than London's, remained loyal for more than forty years. Both seem to have recruited most of their readers among the working people on farms, in the timberlands, and especially in the mines of northern Sweden and the factories of the cities and towns of twentieth-century industrial Sweden. These working people had already successfully tested their newly found political and economic strength, and they prided themselves as doers, not thinkers. They adored the rebellious, expatriate Strindberg whom, it was said, Swedish upperclass respectability had crucified. They wanted no mewling decadence or bookish gloom in their reading, but action, adventure, and sunny romance. London and Sinclair filled their measure to overflowing, for they supplied all these and in addition an explicit sympathy with their socialist causes. Both writers became immediately popular, but both were without influence on those who formulated and kept alive the Swedish animus against America. London and Sinclair, it is true, were critical of America, but neither became in Swedish eyes the critic Hamsun had asked for, for quite apart from their possible qualifications for the role, the kind of reader to whom the two novelists most strongly appealed was simply not interested in America's future Coming of Age—or in much of anything else in America except as it provided numerous useful examples of the evils of capitalism and exciting stories of the Wild West. The writers and critics who fretted over America's shortcomings and who were a few years later to become responsible for Sinclair Lewis's reception, showed no interest in London or Sinclair and seemed quite unaware of their great popular success. At least, they remained silent on the subject, so that we are required to trace the Swedish reception of London's and Sinclair's books mainly in unsatisfactory brief notices or the reviews of enthusiastic amateur critics in the provinces.[2]

[2] The feminist Ellen Key, then nearing the end of her controversial career, was a notable exception to the usual indifference of influential critics toward London and Sinclair. She saw in Upton Sinclair's books signs of a spirit in American culture different from that described in the received Swedish view. Her review of Sinclair's work, "Upton Sinclair och freden," *Frihet*, no. 10 (1918), pp. 3—4, began: "Along with Jack London, Upton Sinclair has also become one of the authors most admired by Sweden's Social Democrats. European—and not least, Swedish-European—stupidity and conceit has many monstrous things to relate about America. They all go on the assumption that America entirely lacks any fine culture, any real literature and art, any philosophy and religion, and that the only God worshiped there is the dollar.... It is not my purpose here to disprove all these ignorant prejudices..." and she concluded with an approving analysis of Sinclair's criticism of America.

The first of London's books to appear were *The Call of the Wild* (mistranslated as *Skriet från vildmarken*—"the call from the wilderness"—and in later editions as *Vildmarken kallar*—"the wilderness calls") and *The Son of the Wolf*. Two years later, in 1909, *White Fang* appeared, in addition to second editions of the first two books, two editions of *The Sea-Wolf*, and two of *Before Adam*. The Jack London vogue was well under way. In a 1915 newspaper account of the previous year's activities in informal adult study groups sponsored by the government, Jack London was listed as the author most frequently requested from the library of 155,000 books provided the study groups' 939 members: "Jack London (500 books), Strindberg (175), Forsslund (140), Selma Lagerlöf (125)...."[3] and so on down the list for twenty-four more names when Mark Twain appears in the 30—50 book group, the only other American on the list. In a review of *The King of the Klondyke* in the previous year, an enthusiastic reviewer had written: "Lord knows how many books Jack London has written; his production is enormous. Have you never read anything by him?—incredible! You must do so at once!"[4] The vogue continued undiminished for twenty years; by 1927, when it began to slacken, fifty-five separate London titles had appeared in nearly 250 editions. Bohlin & Co. was responsible for most of this output, but fourteen other publishers had also taken their share. Most frequently published in those years were *The Call of the Wild* (14 editions), *White Fang* (14), *A Daughter of the Snows* (12), *The People of the Abyss* (11), *Before Adam* (11), *The God of his Fathers* (11), and *The Sea-Wolf* (11). In addition to titles separately published, five "collected" editions (three of them before 1927) have made their appearance in Sweden: a 32-volume edition in 1917–1922 (incorporating some titles separately announced), a 15-volume edition in 1925–1926, a 20-volume edition in 1926–1927, another 15-volume edition in 1929 (paper bound in 1930), and a 16-volume edition in 1939–1940. Such is the record in Sweden of the American author who has been "collected" only once in his own country in a far from complete edition. A survey taken in 1951 of the circulation in Swedish lending libraries of American books places Jack London still very far ahead of all others as the most widely read American author.[5]

Reviews and notices of London's books appeared in newspapers of the cities and provinces, with the provincial critics treating him more seriously

---

[3] "De populäraste författarna," *SvD*, December 4, 1915.
[4] Martin Koch, "'Kungen av Klondyke,'" *Ny Tid*, January 3, 1914
[5] See Appendix C.

than did their metropolitan colleagues. Two strains run through nearly all the notices: first, admiration for London's socialistic bias and his skill as a teller of adventure stories, and second, recognition of the primitive, even naive, quality of both. The socialistic appeal is illustrated in a review of *The Iron Heel:*

> For a socialist it is very heartening that many of the foremost writers of our times not only theoretically adhere to the socialistic point of view but reveal themselves in words and deeds as convinced socialists. It cannot be overlooked that a well-known author, if he joins in the fight for an idea, can do much, in comparison with what we are able. His words and deeds often have a scope and significance that cannot be measured by his contemporaries or determined by the judgment of the future.[6]

Such an author, the reviewer continued, has a great power for good or evil; it is no wonder, therefore, that as a socialist one has the privilege to rejoice at a novel like *The Iron Heel,* for it shows that the most widely read author of the day has clearly turned to socialism. "In this novel he tells us that there is no other salvation from the iron grip of capitalism than the victory of the proletariat under the sign of socialism. Socialism is presented as a necessary consequence of the development of capitalism . . . and [the book] is thoroughly marxistic." It should, he concluded, be in every "People's Library." Another reviewer spoke of London's "social" novels, all of them characterized by a search for the truth, the courage to face life, and a warm feeling for one's fellow man; although not entirely free of "what could be called American sensationalism and advertising," they have something of importance to say to the world.[7]

The emphasis, however, was more frequently placed on the spirit of adventure and the life of action depicted in the books, and it is the colors in London's descriptions, the sense of the exotic and the idyllic which seem more truly to have appealed to the reviewer just quoted than London's views of social problems: "The problem [of proper land cultivation in America] is set in a milieu which delights by its intense colors, taken from the blue sky of summer, the sea of shifting greens and white crests, and gold oranges among the green foliage, the glow of roses and the glory of climbing wisteria." Here, as every critic pointed out, was an uncomplicated view of life with a hearty, ruddy glow of health that warmed the heart and seemed as fresh and invigorating as the outdoors, a char-

---

[6] "Jenki," "Järnhälen," *Verdandisten,* June 12, 1913.

[7] "Rgb," "Bokvärlden," *GHT,* November 19, 1914.

acteristic of London's writing nearly always preferred to any other. "Jack London is strongest and his art of story-telling most fascinating when he interprets the simple and the uncomplicated. . . . [His characters] are people of a wilderness with the atmosphere of a primitive age and of a soundness whose immediacy no one can doubt."[8] Or, more concisely: "The triumph of the good in heart—that defines precisely Jack London's attitude toward life."[9] Such also was the conclusion of the critic who in an excess of admiration compared London with Strindberg and Dostoyevsky, London, after all, being sounder and fresher and less morbid and more appealing with his sobriety and practicality.[10]

Martin Koch, who had espoused the socialist cause in Sweden and was one of the leaders in the new "proletarian" writing of the time, had many strictures to place on *The King of the Klondyke* and other of London's books, but his remarks reveal so plainly London's major appeal in Sweden, and in their exuberance reflect so well the spirit of his acceptance, that they are worth quoting at length. Recognizing the improbabilities in London's narratives and characterizations, Koch at the same time, in accord with his general advocacy of literature by and for the working classes, could welcome London's books as refreshing and bracing for hungry souls weary of the decadence of current Swedish writing with its "bedroom scenes and cultivated eroticism":

> Especially with regard to eroticism, Jack London's books clearly show that their author has grown up in the promised land of the Sunday-schools. That is said without the least intention of malice. It is absolutely clear that in this matter he represents the Americans' boyish chivalry toward woman, who in his consciousness is a curious mixture of high-spirited, robust cow-girl and honey-sweet, lily-white angel. How sound and salutary are not these fundamentally durable views of the complex problems of love! Especially after one has come to be filled with disgust for all the whores of more or less noble extraction encountered in the literature of decadence.
>
> For good or bad, Jack London is American. He represents the new race of the strong, of the primitive man, who, like the author, gladly boast of their "culture" and the "education," while they dispose of those two strange matters in record speed. Nothing in the world prevents these talented people from solving, after a few months' intensive training in math, equations of the fifth degree or other minor matters that make the head of a European spin. Jack London has the American predisposition for strong words, summary reasoning,

[8] "H. E.," "Bland böcker," *Dagen,* September 28, 1915.
[9] B[ror] E[riksson], "Jack London som dramatiker," *Östgöten,* October 20, 1920.
[10] Stellan Engholm, "Jack London: en överblick . . .," *Politiken,* August 30, 1919.

and prompt action. He has also that glorious power, energy, the bright glance of the eyes, everything that speaks directly and irresistibly to the best qualities of the sound and healthy person, to man's manliness and woman's womanliness.[11]

The novel, he continued, is in brief the story of a strong individualist's conversion to socialism, a miracle resulting directly from "a wonderfully naive love story" between the hero and an angelic tomboy. The hero is a darling of the gods and

is as handsome as an American god, with coarse black hair and a smooth-shaven Indian face—golly, girls!—and stronger than any other white man in all of America, Asia, Africa, Australia, and little Europe.... His ability to survive bodily exertions ... can only be compared with his intelligence.... Besides all this, he is a darn nice guy who doesn't like fighting or other nasty things.... The only thing he is afraid of is women. What a man!

And that is Jack London's book, told with astonishing speed and spirit; the suspense is sometimes so strong as to be almost physically painful. And wedding bells ring at the end—read the book! It will do your body and soul good!

In the matter of style, however, the reviewers were less in agreement. Writing about *The Valley of the Moon,* one praised it for displaying "in rich measure all of the author's merits: a fast-moving suggestive style, clear organization, a practical grasp of the problem in question, a pronounced ability to keep his characters alive, and an apparently inexhaustible wealth of striking details."[12] But another found London's style to be so fast-moving as to become "slick journalism,"[13] whereas still another was pleased that there are no long, cumbersome sentences, no wordy explanations:

... no, Mr. Jack is a man who can say a thing in a few concise sentences so that his meaning is clear. For example, he speaks thus about Hawaiian cowboys: "muscular and broad-shouldered, with flashing brown or black eyes and broad regular features, they seem to be as goodnatured, happy, and even-tempered as the climate"—and with that, everything about them has been said. One almost feels that one knows them.[14]

[11] Martin Koch, *op. cit.*

[12] "Litteratur: Jack London," *Soc. Dem.,* December 5, 1914.

[13] Rabenius, "Ny berättelsesamling af Jack London," *Stockholms Dagblad,* September 18, 1915.

[14] Alfr[ed] Kämpe, "Litteratur: En Hawaji-bok av Jack London," *Folkets Dagblad Politiken,* November 11, 1922.

Few, however, were so simple in their demands and many complained loudly of "wordy explanations." A critic quoted earlier in this paragraph balanced his praise with the charge of "astounding naïveté and pretentiousness in presenting rather self-evident things. Jack London's forte is the depiction of primitive beings in primitive nature. His weakness is his theorizing."[15] And this appears to have been the consensus of the more thoughtful critics. When London's Swedish publisher commissioned a book about him, the hagiolatry of the resulting volume[16] offended all critics and evoked this criticism:

> Le Moine's exertions to make someone so obviously engrossed in reality, so animal-like in his soundness, and so intoxicated with life as was Jack London into a philosopher and preacher of new truths, seem almost comical.... It is by no means profundity that makes Jack London what he is; rather it is the absence of it in a vision that looks directly, clearly, and soberly at cherished realities in a delightful world.[17]

Although Jack London's critical acceptance in Sweden, therefore, cannot in the first place be attributed to his socialistic views, which were quickly recognized as naive and which all too frequently resulted in tedious theorizing that few readers could enjoy, the tone set by his anti-industrialism and socialism was emotionally right, especially for a generation of Swedes growing up with the Social Democratic party. His chief appeal lay first in the ease with which he could be read, and secondly in the details and the suspense in stories laid in exotic surroundings of the outdoor world. The themes of his novels, when not cluttered with a dozen or more pet ideas, were certainly not abstruse, the characters were few and their types easily recognized, and to apprehend the exciting nature of the elementary situations comprising his narratives made no serious demand upon his readers. And it was all done with an *élan* that took away any hint of bookishness. The appearance in 1922 of Charmian London's biography of her husband occasioned the sanest comments by a Swedish critic that have come to hand. Birger Mörner's little article defines with conclusiveness the appeal that Jack London had, and still has, for most Swedish readers. Mrs. London's book, Mörner wrote,[18] is far from being definitive or even competent, but it will be widely read. London's death left a vacuum,

[15] "Litteratur: Jack London," *op. cit.*
[16] Osborne Le Moine, *Jack London och hans diktargärning*, Stockholm, 1920.
[17] "B. S—m," "En bok om Jack London," *Lunds Dagblad*, May 8, 1920.
[18] Birger Mörner, "Kring Jack London," *Södermanlands Läns Tidning*, July 1, 1922.

but not because of his contributions to the social problems of our day, for his socialism was "fantastic and faddish," and the paradoxes he liked to toss about were far too shallow to be taken seriously. He was a "natural genius": whatever education he had managed to acquire was really a danger to him as an artist, so that it is his earlier books, which are relatively free of facile theorizing, that will be remembered. Jack London's strength, Mörner summed up, by no means lay in philosophy or world reform, but in "his imaginative power, his extraordinary feeling for nature, his skill in observing the primitive workings of the soul, and his ability to create. Then, too, there was his personality, full of charm—the boyishness and the flaming heart."

Upton Sinclair, as the other well-known contemporary American author writing of social problems, was often coupled with Jack London in the reviews. *The Jungle* was put out by three different publishers in 1906, the edition by Björck & Börjesson running into three printings immediately. It was quickly followed in the same year by *A Captain of Industry*. Sinclair thus preceded London by one year in Sweden. *The Jungle* remains the book Sinclair is best remembered for and is the one most frequently reprinted (10 editions between 1906 and 1945), although from 1917 to 1945 scarcely a year went by without the publication of at least one of his volumes. Only a few, however, have had more than one printing. His socialistic sympathies gave him an instant appeal: "As a writer Sinclair is a full-blooded artist; but he is still more: he is a conscious socialist, a man zealously striving for justice.... No working-class home should be without this exciting, sensational book [*King Coal*]."[19] Moreover, it was said, unlike most "proletarian" writers Sinclair avoided pat situations and stereotyped endings and did not eschew humor.[20] The young author Harry Blomberg, who had already made his debut as one of the first of the new and rising school of "proletarian" authors, wrote in 1920 about *Jimmie Higgins* in the Social Democratic party organ in the northern province of Ångermanland:

> Readers who have read *The Jungle, Samuel the Seeker,* and *King Coal* (and those who have not, should do so) have an equally great respect and admiration for the author as disgust and hatred for American capitalism and its underlings: the state, the press, and the police. It is impossible to put down Sinclair's books with a feeling of indifference. In the first place, they are good, often exciting, novels, carefully wrought and full of fast-moving action. In the

[19] Ernst J. Lundqvist, "Litteratur," *Signalen,* December 7, 1917.
[20] Erik Hedén, "Böcker," *Politiken,* May 25, 1918; and "Upton Sinclairs väldigaste bok," *Soc. Dem.,* December 24, 1919.

second place, his social pathos is so burning and so irresistible that we do not believe anyone could finish reading them without feeling strengthened and confirmed in his socialistic convictions or else without having his eyes opened to socialism.[21]

In general, however, Sinclair's novels, when sympathetically reviewed yet not taken up specifically (as in the last quotation) as testimony on behalf of the socialist cause, were regarded as presentations of the panorama of current events in documentary fashion from a reasonable, rather than the all too frequent crudely doctrinaire point of view. Adverse criticism most frequently leveled at his books spoke of superficiality and a need for greater concentration; a critic of *Samuel the Seeker,* for example, wrote in the Social Democratic *Ny Tid* that the book lacks depth and perspective behind the platitudes, and that the social problem is superficially presented and is solved by oversimplification;[22] a critic of the Communist *Ny Dag* snapped that the "clipping service [Sinclair] subscribes to for his work" neglects the Communist point of view;[23] and elsewhere phrases such as "stereotyped technique" and "contrived situations" crop up in otherwise favorable reviews.[24] Such criticism is reminiscent of the objections made to London's books that the theorizing was superficial or "self-evident," but London's books had the saving grace of his own warm personality and the color of the out-of-doors, and Sinclair never offered him serious competition.[25] And unlike Sinclair, London apparently exercised some literary influence upon a few Swedish authors in the early years of the so-called "proletarian" school, including two such important writers as Dan Andersson and Harry Martinson;[26] Sinclair, on the other hand, seems to have been regarded solely as a brother in the socialist cause and the writer of interesting, informative novels.

[21] H[arry] B[lomberg], "En bok om krig och socialism," *Nya Norrland,* April 10, 1920.
[22] Arvid Rosén, "I samhällets inferno och långt bortom," *Ny Tid,* September 18, 1925.
[23] Edvin E. Persson, "Ny jättevolym av Sinclair," *Ny Dag,* December 6, 1946.
[24] Later criticism made much of these objections; see, for example Alf Ahlberg, "I dårarnas paradis," *DN,* December 6, 1945; Gunnar Brandell, "Politik och spiritism," *GHT,* December 10, 1945; S[ven] B[erger], "År 1939 enligt Upton Sinclair," *SDS,* December 9, 1946.
[25] It is perhaps not too much to say also, since both writers were evidently read chiefly by working people with relatively low incomes, that the price of Sinclair's lengthy books was prohibitive for many who might otherwise have bought them and who could afford London's books.
[26] Schück–Warburg VIII, p. 345, 638.

Twain, Cooper, and Poe of older writers (all of whom were regarded chiefly as authors of books for young people), and Jack London and Upton Sinclair of contemporary authors—such were the chief representatives of American fiction in Sweden during the first two decades of the twentieth century. Moreover, the reputation enjoyed by London and Sinclair is a part of the history of the "proletarian" school of writing in Sweden, an underground movement, so to speak, in creative and critical writing that had yet to make itself reputable in Swedish letters and that was allied in spirit and through individual ties with the political movement of socialism. When it did finally achieve recognition and had indeed all but run its course, other figures, as we shall see, had long since replaced London and Sinclair, and the reputation of American fiction had shifted into an entirely new phase.

CHAPTER III

Swedish Criticism 1920—1930: The Reception of Sinclair Lewis

In the summer of 1921 a Stockholm paper carried a brief notice of the departure for Europe of "the most talked-of author in America today."[1] Before the end of the year *Main Street,* the novel that was causing a furor in the United States, was available in Swedish translation, and the author who was to do more than any other to change the course of American literature in Sweden had appeared on the scene. Between 1921 and 1930, the year of the Nobel Prize, the mood, if not all the convictions, of the critics and public alike with respect to American literature underwent a drastic reversal. For this, Sinclair Lewis's books were greatly responsible. Resistance gave way to receptivity, and American literature acquired for the first time in Sweden the status of a "world literature." The change was not effected of course solely by one author, for Lewis clearly reaped the benefits of the now general interest in America occasioned by the results of World War I, and his contemporaries certainly gave needed substance to the idea of a thriving American literature, but Lewis dramatically introduced that idea in such unequivocal terms that no serious critic dared thereafter neglect the literary wares of "the great land in the west."

The convictions about American culture held by the critics as part of their heritage from Knut Hamsun and their own Swedish writers and as a consequence of their previous experience with American fiction, could lead to only one result when the time came to review the Swedish translation of *Main Street.* Although some did look upon the novel primarily as the story of a man and a woman, not necessarily American, whose different points of view toward life make mutual understanding difficult and even impossible,[2] the most common strain in the reviews emphasized what

---

[1] "Sm," "Författaren för dagen i Amerika," *SvD,* July 29, 1921.

[2] This approach to the book was most notably presented by the editor of the leading daily in western Sweden; T[orgny] S[egerstedt], "En amerikansk boksucccès," *GHT,* April 12, 1922, makes no mention of Lewis's prefatory remarks to *Main Street* in which he

were looked upon as "typical" characteristics of life in an American small town. *Main Street* was for nearly all critics an impressive corroboration by an American writer of what they already "knew" was true of the soul-crushing banality and frustrating spiritual aridity of American life.

The first spokesman of this criticism seems to have been the eminent critic, Ruben Berg, a few years later the author of the first book-length Swedish survey of modern American literature. Lewis's success, Berg wrote, can be compared only with Jack London's; in the present case, however, it is not esthetic qualities that are of consequence, but "the protest, the critical social description, the national satire."[3] Because Englishmen and Americans are more often self-satisfied than self-critical, such a book, Berg continued, will sometimes attract great attention. The best parts of the novel he found to be the scenes and conversations from Gopher Prairie, which "really reproduce this horrible impression [of monotony, tastelessness, and apathy] without in the least seeming like caricature." However, he would not go so far as to call *Main Street* a masterpiece, for he felt it has too much unorganized material, too many side episodes brought in to make the social criticism complete, and this in time becomes tiring and distracting. He concluded on an ominous note already familiar to us: "Nothing could be more different from the Russian creative temperament than the American, but both believe that they shall possess the world, through the force of their size, their countless numbers, and their incalculable natural resources. And it is for us to consider which of them is the least repulsive."

Although these early reviews of *Main Street* were in the main favorable,

extends to a nation-wide scope the satirical purpose and significance of the novel. Segerstedt concluded his review: "It would be worthless to try to answer the question of who was right, he [the doctor] or she [Carol]. They were two different natures. He asks nothing beyond what the town and his work have to offer. She wants to transform and to revolutionize. She is irritated by the philistinism which he thrives in and which is the life blood of the small town.... It is the commonplace in the story, the banal, which has made it so much noticed. Neither the doctor nor his wife is idealized. He is a pleasant and respectable regular sort of fellow, a useful citizen and a competent doctor. She is in many ways a little goose. Still, one is captivated by her abortive efforts to spread her wings. Heaven knows, goose wings are also wings, and she might have been a wild goose.... She is sometimes naive, unthinking, and a little superior, but her unsatisfied longings prevent her from being one of the tame geese."

It became more usual in later criticism to take a similar view; see, for example, Gustaf Olsson, "Sinclair Lewis och kalvinismen," *NDA*, April 7, 1927; and Sven G. Strand, "Amerikanskt," *Soc. Dem.*, July 19, 1927.

[3] Ruben Berg, "En intressant amerikansk roman," *Aftonbladet*, December 5, 1921. Almost identical is "G. J.," "En kritik av Amerika," *SvD*, December 22, 1921.

their praise was also tentative and could be decidedly tepid, and it was not until Lewis's reputation was firmly established in Sweden after the publication of *Babbitt* that critics everywhere took serious notice of that surprising phenomenon, an American iconoclast. *Babbitt* appeared in 1923, and from then until 1930, when Lewis received the Nobel Prize, Norstedt & Söner, Lewis's regular Swedish publisher and ultimately responsible for the introduction of seventeen of the twenty titles by Lewis to appear in Swedish,[4] published a new title of Lewis's every year, in addition to second editions of some and a large third edition of *Babbitt*. Seldom had anything like it been seen in book publication annals since the meteoric rise of Jack London.

Norstedt's advertisement of *Babbitt* called it both "the story of a man, his family, and his one great friendship," and "a masterful portrayal of modern commercial America."[5] As with *Main Street*, however, only a handful of reviewers took the first of these two lines, and all important reviews emphasized the satire of typical American circumstances and character. Nearly all referred their readers to the current view of America as a land without a literature, or worse, a predatory nation soaked in materialism and apparently incapable of a real culture; the observation led either to an expression of satisfaction that an American with the courage needed for the rigors of self-criticism had finally emerged (a hopeful sign, it was universally felt), or to a warning that, since an American had appeared to confirm all that had been most feared about America, the painful truth must be faced. Thus, a long review in a Göteborg paper called *Babbitt* one of the finest examples both of self-criticism of America and of literature that despite Hawthorne, Whitman, and Henry James had heretofore had only a "theoretical existence."[6] The critic of the Social Democratic *Ny Tid* in the same city, although finding more caricature than self-criticism in the book (quite naturally, he explained, because of well-known American characteristics), nevertheless thought the satire so human and psychologically powerful as to raise the novel to the level of art; the

[4] Thall & Carlsson had published *Main Street* but transferred their rights to it to Norstedt for Sw. kr. 800 in June 1926; the second edition of the novel appeared in the following year under the new imprint. Only two works, *Cheap and Contented Labor*, published by Federativ in 1930, and *Gideon Planish*, published by Ljus in 1943, were not introduced by Norstedt, although the latter volume was reissued by them in 1944. As of 1950, the only books by Lewis not translated were *Hike and the Aeroplane*, *The Innocents*, *Jayhawker*, *Cass Timberlane*, and *The God-Seeker*.

[5] *DN*, December 13, 1923.

[6] Einar Nylén, "Det moderna Amerika," *Göteborgs Aftonbladet*, December 21, 1923.

48

portrayal ("the most thorough to date") of Americanism in all its stupidity and inhumanity he considered should be heeded as a warning of the evil consequences of the capitalistic system: "The land of the dollar is a mirror for Europe," the reflection one sees there being "less cheering than monitory and frightening."[7]

In Stockholm, Ruben Berg, reviewing a Lewis novel for the second time, denied that *Babbitt* is caricature, yet he pointed out that the book concerns exactly those things that Per Hallström had written about America so many years before: the terrible pace, the hypocrisy, the rawness, and the egoism of industrialized life, "as though [Berg quoted Hallström as saying] the whole world was running breathlessly, holding on to its sides, in order to be present at a railway accident."[8]

When Fredrik Böök, the pontiff of Swedish criticism of the 1910's and 1920's, turned his gaze upon *Babbitt,* the object of his scrutiny could be certain of a fair drubbing, for he openly shared Per Hallström's views in many things; yet enough was said of a favorable sort that the mere notice of that august person was a guarantee of an enhanced reputation. Professor Böök, who had been elevated to the Swedish Academy the year before, was no ordinary reviewer; a widely read man, he valued the long-range cultural perspective that had its vantage points principally in the German and Scandinavian "classics," yet he was careful not to set his sights too high for the general public, and for them his pronouncements rang with authority. No other literary figure of the time carried so decisive an influence or did more to shape public opinion on cultural topics.[9] A characteristic method of his criticism was to call an impressive roll of pertinent names well-known in various literatures, thence to enter into comparisons and contrasts, to continue with a fairly detailed analysis of the work at hand, and to conclude with a summing-up that had always an air of finality. His criticism, though at times pretentious, could often shed a steady light that other, less discerning criticism lacked. The sensation caused by *Babbitt* could not of course be ignored, and Böök took up the book by first calling attention, as was his wont, to the high praise accorded

[7] Allan Bergstrand, "Babbitt," *Ny Tid,* March 6, 1924.

[8] Ruben Berg, "En ny roman av Sinclair Lewis," *Aftonbladet,* December 20, 1923.

[9] See Schück–Warburg VIII, pp. 23—25. In his analysis of Böök's literary criticism, *Fredrik Böök som litteraturkritiker,* Stockholm, 1939 (Studentföreningen Verdandis småskrifter no. 416), Knut Jaensson says (p. 21) of Böök's reputation: "In sheer number Böök had succeeded in quickly making large conquests of the Swedish public, his power as a critic was considerable, and a favorable review by him resulted almost without fail in several editions."

it by such established writers as John Galsworthy, Hugh Walpole, H. G. Wells, and then continuing with a comparison with a favorite German novel:

> In its attitudes and its intention [the book] has a strong resemblance to Heinrich Mann's *Der Untertan,* and it is not altogether impossible that the American author has received suggestions from the German. In both cases a portrait is sketched which in spite of all its highly individualized details purposes to present a national type; in both cases the author has sought to raise the hopelessly banal to a sort of massive and overwhelming monumentality. Both authors aspire to unsparing candor and revel with Juvenalian bitterness in their portrayal of the low and the mean. But it must be immediately added that Heinrich Mann comes out on top. His Diedrich Hessling is presented with a fierceness, an infernal venomousness, which is utterly perverse; the draught offered by Heinrich Mann is pure sulphuric acid compared with Sinclair Lewis's soft drink. There is only one single scene [Mrs. Babbitt's consolation of her husband when he burns himself] that can be compared with *Der Untertan.* . . . In spite of everything, Sinclair Lewis has a certain cleverly concealed sympathy for his victim, and the conclusion bears an aroma of good feeling. American patriotism cannot be fully eradicated even from a caricature of the average American; it is only a German who can seize on the idea of loathing and abandon every atom of his nature to derision— somewhat like a defendant who applauds the effusions of the prosecuting attorney and in wild rapture begs the jury to disregard all extenuating circumstances. . . . Sinclair Lewis has without the least doubt succeeded in giving an uncommonly graphic, clear, and convincing picture of the average American, of middle class life in the Middle West.[10]

Lewis's style, Böök continued, has something of the photographic factuality of Arnold Bennett's novels. Even the most trivial touches take on documentary worth; Lewis, for example, can give an inventory of Babbitt's pockets so that we get an insight into the whole realm of his experience and habits. Sometimes—as in the scene showing Babbitt on the way to his office, which Böök quoted at length—the novel rises to large vision, when the whole community is seen from a bird's-eye view, and against that background Babbitt, although insignificant as a person, is deeply meaningful as a symbol.

However sympathetically Böök accepted the validity of Babbitt as a representative of the uncultured middle class of America, he could not, however, agree with Lewis's attitude toward Babbittry, and in this matter

[10] Fredrik Böök, "Babbitt," *SvD,* November 26, 1923.

Böök was moved to go one step further than other critics, who for their part were willing to rest with Lewis's implicit standards of value:

> The author seems to feel vaguely that what Mr. Babbitt lacks is culture and individuality, freedom from prejudice, and a liberal mind. If only he could be made a little more radical and unconventional, if only he could be made to think not so well of Sunday school and puritan morality and better of social reform and modern art, he would already have gone a long way toward improvement. Mr. Babbitt feels disowned by the American superman H. L. Mencken and does not know what to make of Butler's *The Way of All Flesh* —it is in such rejected holy writ that Sinclair Lewis apparently expects the salvation of Mr. Babbitt's soul.
>
> On that point Sinclair Lewis has, however, deceived himself. The brilliant Mr. Mencken with all his *Smart Set* can scarcely be expected to exercise any really soothing influence over Babbitt's unnecessary bustling or to have any ennobling effect on his somewhat defective morals. Mr. Mencken has hardly done anything but transfer the rushing, the passion for change, the surface unrest and the dissoluteness from the sphere of material culture to that of spiritual culture; and as we know, it is not with Beelzebub's help that evil spirits are driven out. Should Babbitt become as skeptical and paradoxical as Samuel Butler, he would hardly become any more substantial; he would bluff just as shamelessly and stupidly about expressionism and social criticism as he did before about Sunday school morality and the conservatism that reacts against change, and he would remain the same cheerful and egoistic hypocrite.
>
> When all is said, intellectual revolutions will undoubtedly be of no service to Babbitt, and the puritan tradition in America ought probably to constitute the most suitable and soundest foundation for his cultural development—it has in it various ideals and things of value which he, in his desperate hurry with business and automobiles, has never had time to discover.[11]

Böök's conservative election of the Puritan tradition as the main hope for Babbitt's and America's redemption was of course a departure from the standard Swedish view, but only to strengthen it and not to abrogate any part of it, for to be able to show that America not merely lacked tradition but had also rejected what tradition it had received, was double condemnation. In spite of his indicating some of the weaknesses in Lewis's point of view on a basis different from that of other critics, Böök's formulation of the causes for those weaknesses cannot be said to represent any real revision of the deeply entrenched Swedish attitude toward America.

In the meantime Sinclair Lewis had burgeoned as one of the most

[11] *Ibid.*

popular authors of the day. More than half of the first edition of 2,000 copies of *Babbitt* was sold within a month in a country where a publisher must figure on a total sale of no less than 900 copies on the average to break even with expenses. The second edition, also of 2,000 copies, appeared just four months after the first. By this time interest in Lewis was running so high as to cause the translation and publication of two of his earlier books: *Our Mr. Wrenn* in 1924 and *The Trail of the Hawk* in 1925, both appearing ten years after their respective American publication dates. Both were recognized at once as youthful work but interesting as further revelation of America or of the writer of *Babbitt*. One reviewer praised *Our Mr. Wrenn* for not being the "usual" sort of thing expected from America —no romantic reverie over skyscrapers and gigantic electric signs, and nothing in it of square-jawed brokers or tramps or immigrants—and concluded: "This is a book from the Sunday school of modern puritanism; the schoolmaster is perhaps too obtrusive . . . but the wisdom he preaches is sound and healthy enough: respect for life and the commonplace."[12] Professor Böök also picked up *Our Mr. Wrenn* and discussed it, first, as an early sketch for Babbitt—Mr. Wrenn being really a youthful Babbitt, "the unimpeachable average American"—and second, as a valuable insight into America's *kulturproblem:* "Sinclair Lewis is a master in reproducing the conversational tones and emotional register of shut-in, half-educated Americans in their spasmodic efforts to participate in the mysterious higher culture of which they have heard so much said and about which they dream at the same time they fear and hate it."[13] America seems to look on Europe, he concluded, somewhat as Rome did on "sunken harrowed Hellas."

The Trail of the Hawk came in for unqualified praise by a hack reviewer[14] as a book to be expected of the "great author" of *Main Street* and *Babbitt,* but other, more responsible reviewers took a less enthusiastic view, calling it an early effort and intended mainly as light reading[15] or an interesting book for its early traces of Lewis's later development.[16] The critic of a provincial paper exclaimed at the picture of America given in the book and spoke of Lewis as one of the great exceptions to a literature which "we have not without cause come to regard as literarily and

[12] C[arl]-A[ugust] B[olander], "En amerikansk vardagshistoria," *DN,* November 26, 1924. See also "E. B.," "Grönköping i Newyork," *Göteborgs Morgonpost,* March 14, 1925.

[13] Fredrik Böök, "Amerikanskt," *SvD,* December 5, 1924.

[14] "Gwen" [Else Kleen], "En bra roman," *ST,* October 23, 1925.

[15] I[van] P[auli], "Amerikanskt," *Arbetet,* December 29, 1925.

[16] H[enning] S[öderhiel]m, "Falkens bana," *GHT,* March 9, 1926.

artistically inferior" and in which "we have become used to encounter only banality, sugar-sweet love, and the clumsy realism of adventure stories."[17]

In 1925 Ruben Berg recapitulated his earlier criticism of Lewis in Chapter III of his *Moderna Amerikaner,* the first volume of literary criticism devoted entirely to contemporary American authors.[18] Following the lead of Carl van Doren's *Contemporary American Literature,*[19] from which most of Berg's key ideas and terms were derived, the first chapter of his book discussed the new trend of self-criticism in America and summarized portions of the composite *Civilization in the United States,*[20] which Berg called a "most interesting" example of the cultural and social criticism characteristic of world literature since the war but "hardly anywhere else so striking as in the United States. It would seem that the serious intention to get to the roots of the disastrous tendencies of the recent past will lead it to dig deeper and spread itself further than Europeans have so far shown a willingness for."[21] Berg's second chapter was an introduction to Masters' *Spoon River Anthology* (with selected translations), which he called "the first significant work" of the literary movement that was characterized by the term (van Doren's) "The revolt from the village." The third chapter of *Moderna Amerikaner* was a continuation of this thesis as it applied to Sinclair Lewis; although Masters centered his attack on evil, and Lewis above all ridicules folly and stupidity, both are united in their main viewpoints: "Spoon River and Gopher Prairie will without doubt be regarded henceforth as representative of *the town* or *the village* in the United States during the first two decades of the twentieth century."[22]

Berg's criticism of *Main Street* and *Babbitt* in 1925 agreed in all respects with his earlier newspaper reviews of the two books—they are detailed representations of American life as it really is—although now he allowed himself more room to develop his ideas and to quote significant passages from both books. He noted Carol Kennicott's immaturity for real leadership in reform but agreed on the whole (as Böök, for example, would not) with her point of view; "the experiences Carol Kennicott has and the con-

---

[17] "Arne lbk," "Sinclair Lewis: Falkens bana," *Östgöta Correspondenten,* November 24, 1925.

[18] Ruben Berg, *Moderna Amerikaner,* Stockholm, 1925.

[19] Carl van Doren, *Contemporary American Literature 1900—1920,* New York, 1922.

[20] Harold Stearns, ed., *Civilization in the United States,* New York, 1922.

[21] Berg, *op. cit.,* p. 1.

[22] *Ibid.,* p. 64.

clusions she draws do not seem to be exaggerated or unjust. Lewis has left evidence in rich measure for such a judgment; his book is compact, just as such realistic books in general are whose main point is the depiction of a cultural condition and the criticism of a social class."[23] *Babbitt* takes place in Zenith, a larger version of Gopher Prairie; its hero has reached the critical age of forty-six and "is not only himself but also a symbol for America—he is America with its present anxious fear of being a fiasco."[24] He has been the successful business man and has tried to be the Solid Citizen; he believes in America's spiritual and intellectual superiority, prohibition, democracy, and the efficacy of work.

> Standardized articles take the place for Babbitt of happiness, passion, and wisdom. He himself is a standardized man, with a standardized family and standardized friends; his life is a standardized life with standard virtues and standard sins. We Swedes ought to remember this type from the United States and his history, for we already have him among us, preaching the extraordinary virtues, economic advantages, and spiritual solidarity of standardization. He shouts his mechanistic, materialistic dogmas in a thousand voices, and he convinces constantly increasing numbers that he is the personification of democracy, that he has superseded the romantic anachronism which is called individualism and the classical antiquity which is called intellectualism, both of which are regarded as evils.[25]

And such a life, Berg once more reminded his readers, is what had repelled Per Hallström so violently thirty-five years before.

Berg's chapter on Lewis also included a discussion of *Arrowsmith*, published that same year (1925) in America but not to appear in Swedish translation until the following May. Here was Lewis as a "positive" critic: the hero of his new book, unlike Babbitt, is to be admired. "Martin Arrowsmith has the great quality of wanting to be himself, not to compromise, to be distracted neither for money nor pleasure nor power from that which is his deepest need and passion: science."[26] After sketching in the main points of the narrative, Berg concluded:

> *Martin Arrowsmith* is not Sinclair Lewis's best written work, but it is that which aims the highest. It tries to portray a person for whom the most important thing in life is not outward success, the approval of society, money,

[23] *Ibid.*, p. 67.
[24] *Ibid.*, p. 73.
[10] *Ibid.*, p. 73.
[26] *Ibid.*, p. 77.

propaganda, or being just like other people. Nowhere in the world is this kind of person so uncommon as in the United states, the new idealists and rebels there claim. Martin Arrowsmith is as little an ideal being as his opposite counterpart Babbitt or the little doctor's wife Carol Kennicott, but he represents the struggle to realize the ideal of unselfish work for a great human goal, faithfulness toward one's calling.[27]

Three other critics gave their readers a preview of *Arrowsmith* in 1925 by reporting on the Jonathan Cape edition. One, in Göteborg, praised the novel for unobtrusive, exact knowledge of scientific terms, the fullness of the characterization of the central figure and the excellent portrayal of minor characters like Gottlieb and Sondelius; although at times inclined to be "literary," "the book is absolutely free of pose and is absolutely honest."[28] For somewhat different reasons the critic of *Dagens Nyheter* in Stockholm was also enthusiastic in calling it "a sermon about work, dedicated, passionate, unselfish work—a word of truth on the dollar-continent"; although the "writing is not particularly deep" and "there is nothing remarkable about his characterization and framing of the problem, ... he writes freshly and soundly; there is flesh and blood in his writing. If one compares him with the last American idol, Jack London, one cannot avoid noting the improvement: not only has the form become more literary, but the philosophy of will has in it more culture and humanity."[29] It is of especial interest that a third critic writing of *Arrowsmith* in advance of its Swedish publication was none other than Per Hallström, remembered by Ruben Berg as an early critic of the America satirized by Lewis and respected by the general public as a member of the Swedish Academy.

In reviewing *Arrowsmith* Hallström took occasion to survey Lewis's production to date. His early efforts have their interest, he wrote, but readers would do well to concentrate on his masterpiece *Babbitt* and digest it thoroughly. They should also read Lewis in the original, for no matter how gifted the translator, Swedish "does not yet have the wealth of slang which has sprouted up in the rich earth of the Middle West, and what we do have does not contain the cheerfully bold imagination, the unworried, self-satisfied, and quick vulgarity which is based on widespread,

[27] *Ibid.,* p. 80.
[28] H[enning] S[öderhiel]m, "Amerikansk nutid," *GHT,* April 17, 1925.
[29] C[arl]-A[ugust] B[olander], "En amerikansk läkarroman," *DN,* April 24, 1925.

undiluted, and perfect lack of education."[30] *Babbitt* is Lewis's most important work; in it

> he found the field in which he could make full use of his powers. In this book he has had the rare good fortune to produce, with a talent of considerable but not really great size, a lasting work of art, representative of an entire culture and of a whole epoch—a representation in really living art of a nation's characteristic type, and of precisely that nation which for a long time will perhaps have the most to say in the world.
>
> George Follansbee Babbitt is in himself no great man, but he stands for uncounted millions who resemble each other like berries, with his boyish appetite for life, his buoyant energy, and unfathomable spiritual flatness. His shadow from the western horizon falls on us Europeans grotesquely lengthened, giving us shivers of premonition of what the future will bring. We must look for what little confidence is given us to his redeeming humor, which in the man Babbitt is all the more irresistible as he wins our hearts with all his weaknesses; it is the goodnature and humanity of Lewis's satire which is its most excellent quality.

Arrowsmith, Hallström continued, is still one more attempt "to measure the bedrock and profiles of the American community"; here the conflict is on a higher level and is much sharper. It is a fundamental conflict in America, that

> warm, fat hotbed of democracy, where all the head gardeners tremble with eagerness to pull up the plants in order to show a proud and approving people how magnificently everything grows there. With fiery zeal they strive for the good in life, but most of all they long for applause for making that struggle and the healthy enjoyment of throwing back their heads and shouting out their triumph to the top of the sky with all the wonderfully complicated roar of advertising. In the same way there arises a contradiction in principle between science, naturally fairly quiet and dignified, and the spirit of world reform that exists in noisy and well-meaning humbug.

Lewis, Hallström concluded, has his significance as the foremost literary representative of the present American opposition to the hypocrisy of advertising. "One anxiously waits to see how he will continue his fight.... It appears as if the New World might at last have something new to say for itself, something also which concerns us now more than ever before."

A few days after Swedish readers learned that Lewis had turned down the Pulitzer prize because "like titles, it is demoralizing," *Arrowsmith* appeared in May 1926 in Swedish translation by Margaretha Frölich Odel-

[30] Per Hallström, "Två romaner av Babbitts författare," *SvD,* December 19, 1925.

berg, who was responsible for translating much of Lewis, Dreiser, and other Americans; and two more leading critics were heard from on the subject of Sinclair Lewis. John Landquist wrote that *Arrowsmith,* in revealing the lack of culture in America, goes even further than *Babbitt,* which had presented a terrifying picture of America as "an Inferno of no education, and conventionality supplied with automobiles and standardized ideas."[31] Moreover, Landquist added, *Arrowsmith,* in spite of its markedly American emphasis, is probably the definitive novel about the medical profession. A more restrained review was Algot Werin's in the leading daily of southern Sweden. Lewis's style, he wrote, is like the technique of American films—direct descriptions, palpable realities, rather than moods or reflections. Lewis has a tendency to generalize and even to exaggerate. The character of Arrowsmith is "naive, magnificently naive, as are all the real favorites of Fortune," and the story of his making his way in society is in some respects like the Danish Nobel Prize winner Henrik Pontoppidan's *Lykke-Per.* "Sinclair Lewis is an entertaining and not particularly profound author, but still one to be taken seriously. He is an American and he points up in his way the old wisdom that one cannot at the same time serve both God and Mammon."[32]

Whether as an outstanding novel about the medical profession, the vehicle of sage wisdom, a stirring story of a man's devotion to his ideals, or finally and most frequently, as a true, sharp-tongued, and exciting guide through the jungle of culture-less America, *Arrowsmith* was well received on all sides. What reservations the critics had were not damaging, but they were enough to let *Babbitt* remain in unchallenged first favor. Berg, Bolander, Böök, Hallström, Landquist, Segerstedt, Söderhielm, Werin— scarcely any of Sweden's influential critics had failed to write on Lewis by 1926, and Berg's *Moderna Amerikaner* had put him at the forefront of America's new writers of fiction. *Main Street* in 1921, *Babbitt* in 1923, a second edition of *Babbitt* in 1924, *Our Mr. Wrenn* in 1924, *The Trail of the Hawk* in 1925, *Arrowsmith* in 1926: thus quickly was Lewis building his reputation in Sweden. Also published in 1926 were *Free Air* and *Mantrap,* neither of which got more than polite notices from the critics, one of them so dismayed by the quality of *Mantrap* that he suggested that Lewis perhaps meant the book to be a farce.[33] In the fall of 1927 Norstedt

[31] John Landquist, "En amerikansk läkarroman," *Aftonbladet,* June 17, 1926.

[32] Algot Werin, "Lycko-Per i Amerika," *SDS,* June 3, 1926.

[33] H[enning] S[öderhiel]m, "Äventyr i vildmarken," *GHT,* September 1, 1926. See Appendix B for other reviews of the two books.

brought out Lewis's ten-year-old *The Job,* also generally regarded as negligible, but evoking the following comments, which in effect recapitulate the entire history of Sinclair Lewis's reception in Sweden up to that time:

> Sinclair Lewis may well be regarded as having won a solid popularity in our country. The great American continent steadily continues to attract our interest even if we feel repelled by certain of its cultural manifestations. Lewis has become so interesting to us because although a full-blooded American, he looks at the country and its people with critical eyes—perhaps not altogether as a European, but at any event with wideawake criticism; what he attacks and condemns are often just those aspects of American life and culture which irritate us in the Old World most—undesirable customs that are perhaps explicable by the country's lack of traditions and its amazing technical and economic rise, which has forced interest in spiritual values far into back regions of the soul of the dollar-people.[34]

The book everyone was waiting for, however, was *Elmer Gantry,* which had been creating a nation-wide sensation in America. It appeared in Sweden in 1928, but some critics had again anticipated public interest by reviewing the English edition. This time, many critics protested, Lewis had gone too far and instead of writing a literary work had resorted to exaggeration and outright polemics in a kind of "journalistic *j'accuse.*" Just as Mencken's collection of Americana, although showing

> what rotten eggs can be laid when enthusiastic optimism is joined with expressions borrowed from variants of American advertising and business language, cannot by any means be regarded as typical or representative of American culture, so can *Elmer Gantry* not be taken as a true picture of religion in America. The artist has turned reformer, and he has lost the redeeming feature of all his previous social criticism—sympathy for and understanding of man's efforts to come to rights with a muddled world in order to find some kind of meaning in life. But this is entirely lacking in Gantry. The intention is not to tell of the destinies of the book's characters, but to give religious charlatanry a fatal blow.[35]

Another critic made the same comparison with Mencken and with the same conclusion that for all of Lewis's "photographic and phonographic faithfulness" to his vast collection of material, the *whole* truth is lacking, just as it is in Mencken, who has nothing to say about the more promising

[34] "H. W. L.," "En amerikansk kontorsflicka," *Göteborgs Morgonpost,* October 27, 1927.

[35] H[enning] S[öderhiel]m, "En ny roman av Sinclair Lewis," *GHT,* April 7, 1927.

side of America, its Woodrow Wilsons, Edgar Lee Masters ("who more than most is deserving of the Nobel Prize"), and its Irving Babbitts ("a modern Sainte-Beuve"), Millikan, Carrel, and even Sinclair Lewis himself.[36] Lewis's books, he added, are more caricatures than they are novels, *Gantry* more so than any previous volume.

This and more was also the tenor of a long review in the highly conservative *Nya Dagligt Allehanda* by the critic Knut Hagberg, who felt that "if any books are to be put on the index [of censored books], Sinclair Lewis's *Elmer Gantry* without doubt ought to qualify for first consideration."[37] No matter from what point of view it is a poor book, he wrote, for in it Lewis has left his earlier satire for a "coarse, misplaced, and cheap jest of everything that yet has value in American culture, that is to say, religion." This man, who poses for profile shots before the Louvre as proof of his broad education, has taken as the fundamental thesis of his book the belief "that it is not only stupid, but absolutely criminal to be concerned with such questions as those of sin and salvation, so long as one can be educated into being a gentleman by being photographed in front of famous buildings in Paris." And Hagberg concluded:

> If this had been merely a satirical portrayal of possible anomalies among the independent sects in America, it could indeed be remarked that the satire is astonishingly crude, rancorous, and exaggerated; but the book could possibly have been defended as a reaction against actual conditions. *Now this is not the case.* *Elmer Gantry* is certainly not solely or even primarily a satire of independent sects in the U.S.A. It is programmatic writing, and if it were not absurd to speak of philosophy in connection with Lewis, one could call the book a philosophic novel. It is merely by chance that the independent sects are the object of the author's homeric ridicule. . . . He has a philosophical account to settle with Christianity itself. . . . His book has the deliberate and calculated purpose to arouse contempt for every form of religion, and at the same time the author sneaks like a coward behind the camouflage protection of art. . . . Spiritual life is dangerous ground; for Sinclair Lewis it is *terra incognita* where he has completely lost his way, and in the darkness he has lost, one by one, his capabilities: a sense of decorum, the instincts of a gentleman, and finally his head.

This immoderate, unguarded attack was answered in kind by the Social Democratic *Ny Tid* in a denunciation of Dr. Hagberg which took time out, nevertheless, to remind him of such a peculiarly American phenomenon as

[36] Sten Selander, "U. S. A:s samvete,' *Stockholms Dagblad*, August 15, 1927.

[37] Knut Hagberg, "Sinclair Lewis som religionskritiker," *NDA*, February 19, 1928.

"Jumping Jesus" (Billy Sunday). It defended Lewis's right to use what weapons he could to fight smugness, bigotry, and cheap optimism in the "dollar-land."[38] The reviewer in *Social-Demokraten* also took exception to Dr. Hagberg's criticism and defended Lewis's book as a specific attack on a heretic rather than a general attack on religion. Everything being fair in such a battle, he pointed out that Billy Sunday, Aimee MacPherson, the fundamentalists, and the Ku Klux Klan were enough justification for the kind of exaggeration Lewis was being accused of.[39] Lewis reminded this critic in some ways of Ibsen (Babbitt being a little like Hjalmar Ekdahl, Arrowsmith like Brand, Gantry a bestialized Peer Gynt or, better, Steensgaard in *De unges forbund*) and Maupassant (Gantry being like the central character in *Bel-Ami*). He concluded,

> *Elmer Gantry* is no uplifting book. When you have finished reading this thick volume, you have really become weary of associating with its unpleasant protagonist, and the detailed presentation of the interiors of fundamentalist churches in the long run becomes tiring. The acrimonious protest against unorthodox religious "bunk" and commercialism also disturbs the literary impression. The story is not lacking in artistic values; many of its scenes are powerfully dramatic, even gripping ... and Gantry himself is a significant psychological study—he belongs ... among the permanent figures in world literature ... [but the novel] is less a work of art than a cultural document.[40]

And this was how the case of *Elmer Gantry* finally came to rest, once the intramural quarrels of the critics were forgotten.

The Man Who Knew Coolidge, also translated in 1928, created no such sharp disagreement, however; nearly every critic admired Lewis's ear for nuances in American slang and jargon, called Lowell Schmaltz a new Babbitt, "the incarnation of the whole of 100 % pharasaitical Comstock-

---

[38] Harry Borglund, "Littcraturkritik ur befordringssynpunkt," *Ny Tid*, February 25, 1928. *Ny Tid's* own review of the novel—Melker Johnsson, "Amerikansk självprövning," April 5, 1928—was a much more modest appraisal but supported the earlier defense of *Elmer Gantry* by citing Per Hallström's and Henning Berger's bitter portrayals of America, the case of Billy Sunday and Bruce Barton's interpretations of Christ as an advertising man, and Mencken's corroborating evidence, although the critic felt that the bitter tone of the book did tend to spoil it as a work of art.

[39] I[van] P[auli], "Själasörjaren från Kansas," *Soc. Dem.*, March 25, 1928.

[40] *Ibid.* "S. V.," "*Elmer Gantry,*" *Arbetet*, March 1, 1928, is also a protest against Hagberg's review but defends the novel without qualification, as did also Artur Lundkvist, "Ulv i fårakläder," *Arbetaren*, February 20, 1928, which has additional interest in being one of the earliest notices of an American book by the critic who was soon to play a leading role in introducing American literature to Sweden.

culture"[41] or something equally sinister, but found in general that the unrelieved monologue, although a kind of virtuoso performance, was pretty dull. In addition to publishing *Elmer Gantry* and *The Man Who Knew Coolidge* in 1928, Norstedt also launched an edition (the third) of 30,000 copies of *Babbitt,* an extraordinarily large edition by Swedish standards. What their German-Swiss neighbors had to say about Lewis was of course of interest to the Swedes, and Kriesi's book on Lewis was reviewed that year;[42] the only previous biographical account of Lewis, aside from information derived from American sources, had been Lewis's own sketch of his life and writing in Norstedt's annual *P*A*N*.[43] The special Sunday section of *Svenska Dagbladet* ran a series of eleven articles by Lewis on his travels in England that same summer,[44] and still in a dominant position to mold public opinion in literary matters, Fredrik Böök wrote a series of three major articles on Lewis for the same paper earlier in the year.[45]

[41] Carl-August Bolander, "President Coolidges klasskamrat," *DN,* May 16, 1928. For additional reviews of *The Man Who Knew Coolidge,* see Appendix B.

[42] Bror Olsson, "Sinclair Lewis," *NDA,* June 6, 1928, emphasized the biographical content of Hans Kriesi, *Sinclair Lewis,* Frauenfeld, 1928.

[43] Sinclair Lewis, "Självporträtt," trans. Margaretha Odelberg, in *P*A*N: vers och prosa,* Stockholm, 1927, pp. 63—77.

[44] Sinclair Lewis, "Mr. Babbitt i England," *SvD,* July 8, 15, 22, 29; August 5, 12, 19; September 2, 9, 16, 23, 1928.

[45] Fredrik Böök, "Sinclair Lewis," *SvD,* April 15, 22, 29, 1928. After likening Lewis to Cervantes, Dickens, Goncharov, and Daudet, and giving some biographical information, Böök took up Lewis's work book by book. *Our Mr. Wrenn* is a little book but distinguished by "the virtuosity with which Lewis presents the various jargons of the uneducated, the half-educated, and the driveling esthetic snobs." There is an undercurrent of "an intense feeling of being ill at ease in the American milieu, crowded, banal, poor in spirit, and of a longing just as intense for ... the refinements of European culture." *The Trail of the Hawk* is less original, but it is important in bringing Lewis closer to his real work of social criticism. Dr. Frazer is modeled after Mencken, Lewis's "master and teacher," who has served America as Georg Brandes served Scandinavia in drawing its attention to continental literature. "America at the present time is obviously at the same point of development as were Denmark and the Nordic countries at the end of the 1870's and early 1880's. Religious orthodoxy has begun to lose its power, national self-sufficiency has received a blow.... Religion is criticized, society is attacked; one assaults marriage, principles of education, all authorities and conventional ideas." *The Job* is a minor work, as is *Free Air,* though less pretentious than the former. Böök's judgment of *Main Street* is not unexpected: Lewis is writing about the specifically American town which has no history, no tradition (unlike European towns), for the older traditions of the Pilgrims and of Franklin and Emerson have been interrupted, and later immigrants have by social pressure been forced to lose their Old World ways. Lewis implies that American culture suffers from a lack of European radicalism, but would it not be more correct, Böök asks,

In reviewing Lewis's production from *Our Mr. Wrenn* to *Elmer Gantry*, Böök had many strictures to make, so that finally only *Babbitt* stood free of any serious charges, with *Main Street* as a second choice. Nevertheless, Böök so clearly revealed a real admiration for Lewis's technique—his masterly handling of significant details and his ability to capture the right tones of speech in his dialogues—that the target of Lewis's satire became for once almost a secondary matter. But even Böök's survey differed very little from the typical criticism, which welcomed Lewis as a clear-eyed, sharp-tongued satirist of the interior workings of the bewildering, sprawling country to the west—the "real" U.S.A. *Elmer Gantry* was, of course, the occasion for Böök's and Hagberg's greatest deviation from the usual critical approval of Lewis's methods, for in this book, they felt, the satire had moved over into holy ground that was to be defended at all costs for its traditions. The leftist critics had naturally little use for such a point of view, and they were in the majority.

The Swedish appearance of *Dodsworth* in the fall of 1929 had been anticipated by many months in nearly every leading newspaper, whose critics reported as early as March on the English or American editions. With the exception of Ruben Berg, who felt the book to be a failure to fulfill the promise of *Elmer Gantry* and earlier books because of its "crying need for concentration, tighter construction, stronger lines,"[46] the critics

to say that it lacks European conservatism? In his criticism of *Babbitt,* Böök emphasizes, as he had done earlier, Lewis's humor in portraying Babbitt and his ability to give thousands of details without burdening his writing. It is, he states, Lewis's greatest book. *Mantrap* is merely a repetition of *Free Air. Arrowsmith* and *Elmer Gantry* are grand attempts at a "broad, exhaustive, and at the same time synthesized social description"; they could have been given the titles "Science in America" and "Religion in America" respectively. The former tells much about the level of medical training and practices in America; its weak point is Lewis's romantic conception of pure science—he forgets that medicine is a practice as well as a science—and he feels compelled to use non-Americans, one a German Jew and the other a Swede, to present that science, but both are "romantic postulates" and not clearly defined, credible characters. *Gantry* is the unpleasant variation of *Babbitt,* as *Arrowsmith* was the pleasant. Gantry "has the eagerness, the energy, the undeveloped intellectuality of Babbitt; but the diffuseness, the deficiency in self-knowledge have been developed in Gantry to hypocrisy, unprincipled duplicity; selfishness has grown to ruthless unscrupulousness, vanity to delusion." There is no denying that religion in America has been commercialized, but Lewis's picture seems too one-sided. Unlike *An American Tragedy, Gantry* does not even once present a scene or character to show what religion means for the weak and deficient, or what a sincerely religious person is like. The book is crudely polemical and lacks nuances, and Böök wishes that Lewis had attacked the really big threat: advertising and the press.

[46] Ruben Berg, "En ny roman av Sinclair Lewis," *Aftonbladet,* October 24, 1929.

praised *Dodsworth* as a renewal of the early Lewis, the more evenly balanced, good-humored, yet satirical Lewis of *Babbitt* and *Arrowsmith*. But there was some division of opinion as to whether the book was primarily a satirical travel book containing many subtle insights and acute observations about America and Europe,[47] or the story of a more intelligent, more modest Babbitt and his light-headed wife.[48] Dr. Georg Svensson called it both, reminding his readers that Lewis did not have his reputation merely because "he's the man who writes nasty things about America"; *Dodsworth* "is first of all a story about human beings, or rather about two, but at the same time it discusses countless timely topics, mostly of course America and especially America vs. Europe."[49] Professor Böök also called it both a novel and travel reporting, but unlike Dr. Svensson, Böök criticized the two "parts" as though they were indeed divisible and separate entities; the story of the marriage is well told, he wrote: "The pleasure-greedy, coldly calculating and at the same time childishly undeveloped Anglo-Saxon type of woman is taken to a T.... The whole portrayal [of Fran] breathes an obvious bitterness toward modern emancipated woman. We are now far from the sentimental, chivalrous feminism" of the early novels.[50] The "journalistic" part of the novel is not profound analysis, Böök continued, but Lewis in *Dodsworth* is unusually free of prejudice, and his observations of Europe and America are not snobbish, easy generalizations; rather, they have the frankness and honesty which are the most appealing of American characteristics when free of aggressiveness. Whatever emphasis, however, was put on *Dodsworth,* Lewis seemed for most critics to have been restored after the dubious years of *Mantrap, The Man Who Knew Coolidge,* and *Elmer Gantry,* which were now regarded either as unfortunate lapses that any great author is subject to, or (in the case of *Elmer Gantry*) polemical writing perhaps not worthy of the master, yet a justifiable contribution to a current cultural controversy in America.

From the appearance of *Main Street* in 1921 to *Dodsworth* in 1929, Lewis had built up in Sweden a reputation that allowed both book reviewers and publishers at the end of the period to hail him with impunity as "the best known author of modern American literature" at a time when America had become "the most interesting country in the world,"

[47] H[enning] S[öderhiel]m, "Sinclair Lewis' nya roman," *GHT,* March 25, 1929; Axel Larsson, "Sinclair Lewis' nya skarpa samhällssatir," *SDS,* October 17, 1929.
[48] Carl-August Bolander, "Mister Babbitt i Europa," *DN,* April 3, 1929.
[49] Georg Svensson, "Mannen som Babbitt ville lära känna," *NDA,* March 20, 1929.
[50] Fredrik Böök, "Amerikaner i Europa," *SvD,* April 2, 1929.

and American literature the most exciting of all foreign literatures. At times critics had berated him for superficiality both in characterization and in satire, but the fact remained that he had created Babbitt and had told truths surprising on the lips of an American. In their essentials, these truths, as many critics had pointed out, were those promulgated earlier by Hamsun, Hallström, Berger, Hellström, and others. They and Lewis alike, each in his own way, denounced America as a land serenely unaware of its intellectual poverty, wonderfully contented with its material superiority, and fired with a zeal, in the name of humanitarian idealism, to reduce the rest of the world to its own meager spiritual proportions. Lewis of course made no mention of any physical dangers of life in America and was happily free of the brooding melancholy typical of the Swedish writers. Certainly he would never have subscribed to the savage, sweeping condemnation of America by Knut Hamsun. But in those respects in which he did seem to corroborate earlier criticism, he was far more detailed and objective, hence far more convincing and authoritative. Moreover, as the critics said of all his books except *Elmer Gantry,* he wrote apparently out of love and not personal disappointment or rancor and was for this reason more "balanced" and "good-natured" than his Scandinavian predecessors.

Thus there seemed after all to have arisen in barbaric America, despite Hamsun's skepticism that there ever would, "one little doubter," "one seeker of light," "one spirit in rebellion" to undermine the smugness that had enraged Hamsun and that Hallström had called the greatest defect in the American character.

CHAPTER IV

Swedish Criticism 1920—1930: The Reception of Lewis's Contemporaries

Sinclair Lewis did not, of course, fight a lone battle in gaining Swedish acceptance of his books. He shared the benefits of a sharp rise of general interest in American literature, itself a result of the sudden displacement in popular favor of Germany, for many years the predominant foreign influence upon Swedish tastes and institutions, by the new world power in the west. Whereas Norway had for long been oriented toward England and the west, and Denmark's strongest cultural ties were with France, Sweden had for many years looked upon the new Germany of Bismarck and the Kaiser as its geopolitical brother, and its universities, its army, and even much of its early socialism were patterned upon German models. World War I did much to dampen that ardor, probably less for the older generation of Swedes reared in respect for Germanic institutions and literature as cultural manifestations romantically related to their own, than for a rebellious younger generation anxious to establish its independence by aligning itself with whatever was new and even a little shocking. Certainly the indifference of the Swedes to American culture before the war served now to whet their curiosity, and everything American soon became fashionable, though not without causing dismay in the hearts of many who saw in the shift of enthusiasm from Germany to America a dangerous abandonment of cherished values. All the reviews, for example, of a travel book on America sounded the same wry note on the sudden change of heart in Sweden toward America; as one critic wrote:

> For long have we fine old gentlemen of Europe looked with superiority on the great pioneer country on the other side of the Atlantic. For it was not precisely the European upper classes who embarked for over there; to put it bluntly, it was the lower classes—and for us the U.S.A. became a kind of slum quarter on the outskirts of our high-born European civilization.
>
> Then one morning we awaken from the bloody night of war to stare at the ruins of what was once proud Europe, and an uneasy thought begins to

haunt us: Could it possibly be that it is we who live on the wrong side of the tracks? ...

The problem of America is too intimately tied in with our own cultural problem for it not to have forced our attention upon it. It isn't only our poverty-stricken noblemen who have crossed the Atlantic to play Indians with the pioneers; ever more strongly has the interest grown in Europe in conditions over there, and American culture and literature have come into focus.[1]

Popularly, the most striking sign of the new focus on American culture was, for better or worse, the movies. Despite a vigorous native film industry and easy accessibility to lively sources on the continent, the movies being shown in Sweden were overwhelmingly American, starring such favorites as Irene Rich, Mary Pickford, Tom Mix, and Charlie Chaplin. On the other hand, the legitimate theater being confined largely to Stockholm and Göteborg, the rise of interest in American drama was not as perceptible, but it was not long in the 'twenties before Eugene O'Neill was becoming one of the most widely discussed of contemporary dramatists.[2] Still more difficult to appraise is the correlation between the reception of American poetry and the rise of general interest in America, for although the evidence is relatively meager and widely scattered, the impressions which the poetry made upon individual readers could evidently be quite deep. Whitman had been noticed long before the 'twenties, yet it was not until then that his poetry began to appear with any frequency and not until the 'thirties that his influence on Swedish writers was clearly felt.[3]

[1] Carl-August Bolander, "Problemet U. S. A.," DN, December 5, 1927. Similar sentiments are expressed in Johan Mortensen, "Intryck från nuets U. S. A.," SDS, December 21, 1927; Lydia Wahlström, "Det 'gamla' Amerika," Svenska Morgonbladet, December 27, 1927; I[van] P[auli], "Amerikanska perspektiv," Soc. Dem., December 20, 1927; and Carl G. Laurin, "Amerikanismen," SvD, December 19 and 20, 1927; all of which are reviews of Anna Lenah Elgström's and Gustaf Collijn's U. S. A.: Liv och teater, Stockholm, 1927.

[2] Ruben Berg, "Förenta staternas moderna dramatik," Aftonbladet, April 3, 1922, reports the staging of Clyde Fitch plays in Stockholm as early as 1911, but it was O'Neill, the Nobel Prize winner for literature in 1936, who created a Swedish audience for American drama; his Anna Christie was published in translation in 1923 and was soon followed by The Emperor Jones, The Hairy Ape, and others.

[3] The earliest notice in Sweden of Whitman seems to be Andrea Butenschön, "Walt Whitman," Ord och Bild, XIV (1905), 251—267, which includes a few translations. Articles on Whitman and translations of his poetry in the 'twenties include H[a]g[a]r O[lsson], "Walt Whitman föregångaren," Ultra, I (October 15, 1922), 44—45 (accompanied by translations by Elmer Diktonius on pp. 36 and 45); Walt Whitman, "Som om en vålnad smekte mig," trans. Elmer Diktonius, Ultra, I (November 30, 1922), 89; and Walt Whitman, "Grunden för all metafysik," trans. Karin Boye, in Hardarna, Stockholm, 1927, pp. 73—74.

As a result perhaps of the leading position given Edgar Lee Masters in Ruben Berg's *Moderna Amerikaner* and in a volume of American poetry translated by the Swedish-Finnish poet Elmer Diktonius, *Spoon River Anthology* probably did more than any other single collection to awaken interest in modern American poetry, which in the 'twenties was appearing regularly for the first time in slim volumes of verse and short-lived magazines.[4]

Fiction, however, was streaming in, and American novels, good and bad, appeared side by side in bookstore windows. Near the end of the decade one writer protested against the "foreign trash" displayed in the window of a Stockholm bookstore, although the shop next door contained a more respectable company ("if one is to believe publishers' advertisements"): Theodore Dreiser, Willa Cather, Sherwood Anderson, Sinclair Lewis, and other Americans, "for," as the writer sarcastically added, "all these geniuses belong to the great republic."[5] Certainly it was true that Mark Twain, Cooper, Poe, Jack London, Upton Sinclair, and a miscellany of some three dozen other authors published in the years before 1920 were no longer enough to satisfy the rapidly growing interest in American fiction, and between 1920 and 1930 one hundred additional authors were introduced in Swedish translation.[6] Two-thirds of these new authors made only single appearances, and the books of only ten of them (including of course Sinclair Lewis) went collectively into more than five editions. But there were many

---

[4] In addition to translations of Masters, translations of Pound and Sandburg appeared in Elmer Diktonius, *Ungt hav,* Helsingfors, 1923; of Masters, Lindsay, Scudder, Middleton, Teasdale, Untermeyer, and Alan Seeger in Karl Asplund and Gunnar M. Silfverstolpe, *Vers från väster: Modern engelsk och amerikansk lyrik i svensk tolkning,* Stockholm, 1922; of E. E. Cummings ("La Guerre" and "Impression") by Artur Lundkvist in *Quosego: Tidskrift för en ny generation,* No. 4 (1929), pp. 197—199. Criticism of Masters in the 'twenties may be found in Ruben Berg, *Moderna Amerikaner, op. cit.,* and in Klara Johanson, "Amerikanska rebeller," in *Det speglade livet,* Stockholm, 1926, pp. 215—232.

[5] Anna Lenah Elgström, "Babbitt erövraren," *Soc. Dem.,* November 3, 1928. A few years later Viveka Starfelt-Hallgren, "Amerikansk kulturimport," *Fönstret,* No. 9 (February 28, 1931), p. 4, inveighed against the flood of "true stories" from the dollar-country appearing in the Swedish weeklies (even in that stolid family journal *Smålänningen!*). A reply appeared a few weeks later by "J. B. H.," *ibid.* (March 14, 1931), p. 14, pointing out that the variety of magazines in America had no parallel in Sweden and that it was the preoccupation of the Swedish magazines with the "true story" type that gave the impression that little else was available from America. In the depression year of 1932, the cry against American stories was sounded again by Per Nilsson-Tannér, "Köp svenskt—läs amerikanskt!" *Fönstret,* No. 12 (March 9, 1932), p. 6.

[6] See Appendix A.

old favorites among the new to minister to the wants of a growing reading public. American adventure stories, Westerns, and books for boys and girls found a ready market: books by Rex Beach, for example, ran into 13 editions in this period, Edgar Rice Burroughs 26, James O. Curwood 31, Zane Grey 7, Archibald Gunter (a mysterious stranger from the 1890's, the author of such juveniles as *The Adventures of Dr. Burton, Don Belasco of Key West, Her Senator,* and dozens of others) 58, William J. Long 14, Jean Webster 9, Fred White 7, and the Pennsylvania-born Baroness Hutten 5. Stories by writers like Peter B. Kyne were becoming well known as well as a host of "whodunits." The publishers' search for popular fiction led to the successful resuscitation of the novels of David G. Phillips (of *Susan Lenox* fame) and the publication in 1924 of the then 44-year-old *Ben Hur* by Lew Wallace. Edna Ferber began a long and steady career in Sweden with *So Big* in 1925, *The Girls* in 1926, and *Show Boat* in 1927. Kathleen Norris, first translated in 1917 and frequently translated in the 'twenties, was replaced before the end of the decade by such writers as Temple Bailey and Fannie Hurst.

In sheer quantity, the translations of these writers constituted the main stream of the "flood" of American fiction that spilled over into Sweden during the 'twenties. It was a stream that ran in wellworn and not very deep channels. Occasionally, however, critics discovered writers to pause before and even to ponder. The most important of these included, of course, Sinclair Lewis, but also Sherwood Anderson, Edith Wharton, and Theodore Dreiser. Four other writers, Upton Sinclair, Joseph Hergesheimer, Ellen Glasgow, and Willa Cather, also received special notice during the 'twenties, but the critics soon disposed of them as competent, even at times excellent, novelists of little significance.

Upton Sinclair had by the 'twenties assembled a loyal group of readers in Sweden; his books were appearing in second and third editions and ten more were added to Holmström's list during the decade, including *Oil!*, which quickly ran to three editions. The novels still were seriously read and acclaimed, however, almost solely for their significance in the socialist cause. His work was suggestive, it was said, of the possibilities for self-criticism in America, but rarely did it receive more than the faint praise of "interesting," "informative," or "documentary." His themes were timely and were certainly pleasing to a growing group of socialist readers increasingly aware of their political power, but the writing was generally felt to be more fluent than penetrating, and the results were decidedly not great art.

Joseph Hergesheimer, on the other hand, as an American of artistic pretensions, took many reviewers by surprise, who were pleased to see that not all American literature, as one said, consists of "wild-west, dollar-chasing best-sellers." Hergesheimer's first book to be translated, *Java Head* in 1921, elicited a review from Olle Holmberg, soon to become an essayist and critic of note, in which he praised the novelist's ability to marshal details and to give finely wrought, knowledgeable descriptions of interiors of rooms and houses, but deplored Hergesheimer's neglect in characterization—a neglect that makes "his characters seem as empty as his rooms are full."[7] In all, five books by Hergesheimer were published in Sweden, the first in 1921, the last in 1926, when *The Bright Shawl* appeared with an introduction by the poet and member of the Swedish Academy, Anders Österling. One reviewer called the book a Cuban water-color and surmised that its author had been schooled in the French masters.[8] Another, calling Hergesheimer a fine artist, sensitive and appealing if not very original, supposed that his chief European model had been Joseph Conrad, and added, in appreciation of Hergesheimer's sensitivity: "Hergesheimer does not allow young Charles Abbott to be disappointed in Cuban reality. It is rather the old bachelor who in his dreams of times gone by suddenly sees reality as it was, under the influence of his nephew's disillusionment. This carefully executed concept contributes toward giving the story its peculiar, half unreal, half intensely experienced character."[9] Hergesheimer reminded still another critic of Flaubert,[10] and another pronounced the novel "not a factory-made product from America, as one might suspect since it is a best-seller there, but a work of art, color, and poetry."[11] But for all his acclaimed artistry, Hergesheimer could not escape the charge of being a romanticist: he was not one of the "moderns," a social critic.

Ellen Glasgow, bearing an honored name in American literary history, made even less impression upon Swedish critics than did Hergesheimer; so little serious attention did she receive, indeed, that it is admittedly questionable whether the reception accorded her novels admits of inclusion here. A reviewer of *The Romantic Comedians*, the only one of her novels to be translated in the 'twenties, assumed the author (who had been in print since 1897) to be making her debut in 1926 and praised the daring

[7] Olle Holmberg, "'Ammidons hus,'" *NDA*, May 1, 1921.
[8] Gabriel Jönsson, "En artistisk amerikan," *SDS*, September 13, 1926.
[9] H[enning] S[öderhiel]m, "Kubansk romantik," *GHT*, August 26, 1926.
[10] Kj[ell] S[trömber]g, "Exotisk frihetsromantik," *ST*, September 14, 1926.
[11] Carl-August Bolander, "Ny översättningslitteratur," *DN*, October 20, 1926.

and boldness of a young person in tackling such a difficult theme with "pleasing grace" and in bringing to the task a surprisingly vast knowledge of people.[12] When *They Stooped to Folly* appeared in 1930, it was welcomed as an unusually enjoyable book about everyday life in England.[13] Her later books did not fare much better, and in fact her Pulitzer prize-winning *In This Our Life* was generally regarded as disappointing in its prolixity and ponderous psychologizing.[14]

Although Willa Cather held a higher place in critical and popular esteem than did Ellen Glasgow from the very beginning, when *O Pioneers!* was translated in 1919, her work received in the 'twenties little more than polite notices of its "quiet," "sober," or "worthy" "epic style."[15] Once more it was Ruben Berg in his self-appointed task of taking up the cause of American writers who was first ready to try to give Willa Cather her due. His long notice of *The Professor's House*, translated in 1925, was chiefly sympathetic synopsis, but it concluded: "Willa Cather's book, with its exquisite, measured narrative, its fine, sensitive character portrayal, is fascinating reading and a work of art of high rank."[16] It was not, however, until the 'thirties, when Lewis had pocketed the Nobel Prize in the name of American literature, that the critics began to treat Cather's novels as important literature. As one reviewer put it, on the occasion of the publication of the London edition of *Shadows on the Rock* in 1931, in spite of four translations into Swedish, Willa Cather

---

[12] "R. S—g," "Amerikanskt vardagsliv," *SDS*, December 21, 1928.

[13] "K. H—g," "Nutida engelskt familjeliv," *Göteborgs Morgonpost*, November 27, 1930.

[14] "V. N.," "En familjetragedi," *SvD*, September 10, 1942; A[nders] Ö[sterling], "Amerikansk prisroman," *ST*, September 24, 1942; and Rune Andhé, "En prisroman om vår tids människor," *Göteborgs Morgonpost*, October 7, 1942. Two much more favorable reviews, which thought the prolixity largely counteracted by excellent characterization, were: "... el," "Tre amerikanska författarinnor," *Arbetet*, September 26, 1942; and H[enning] S[öderhiel]m, "En klok bok," *GHT*, June 12, 1943.

[15] The epithets were applied to nearly all her books but were not enough to establish an independent reputation; because of the Midwestern locale of many of her novels, she was tirelessly and unfavorably compared with Sinclair Lewis. *O Pioneers!* was little more than a fine book about Swedes in America, and such also was the kind of praise given *My Ántonia*.

[16] Ruben Berg, "Willa Cathers nya roman," *DN*, April 11, 1926 (and in shortened form in *Aftonbladet*, November 20, 1927). Other reviewers of the same novel complained at length of the composition of the book, calling it "slack and superficial" with "unmotivated development" and "obvious lack of proportion": "Gwen" [Else Kleen], "Amerikansk missroman," *ST*, November 9, 1927; and "M. N.," "En amerikansk familjefar," *GHT*, November 14, 1927.

has not won a name among us as have her countrymen, Lewis and Dreiser, not to mention other Americans ... [she is American in a different sense:] I hardly believe there is a single skyscraper in her books, nothing of that "bigness" which—especially in recent years—has aroused the curiosity and almost romantic wonderment of the Swedish reading public. Neither does she allow us to feel so happily superior as we did when Lewis introduced Babbitt. Her books beat no big drums; neither do they have the breadth of Dreiser's volumes. They nevertheless display a narrative art and a psychological understanding which rank at the top of what contemporary literature can offer.[17]

Although Sinclair, Hergesheimer, Glasgow, and Cather gained only secondary positions at the most in the esteem of the critics, they and a few others, like Floyd Dell, John Erskine, and of course the older writers, like Cooper, Hawthorne, and Twain, whose books were being regularly reissued, secured the notice of the public often enough to contribute materially to its awareness of an American fiction with serious literary pretensions. The task of the critics was subsequently made that much easier when they came to invite their readers to consider the merits of such novelists as Edith Wharton, Sherwood Anderson, Theodore Dreiser, and Sinclair Lewis. The work of these four elicited reviews and critical essays from every important Swedish critic of the 'twenties. By the end of the decade, their work came to be regarded as a formidable contribution to world literature. The reputation of Sherwood Anderson, it must be added at once, was short-lived, yet in 1928 his was a name to be seriously reckoned with and, as we shall see, critical expectations for a few years ran high that from him would come perhaps some of the very best of the new American fiction. The reputations of the other three, Wharton, Dreiser, and Lewis, were on much firmer footing, but it became conventional to compare all four writers with each other as though they were a select company capable of conjuring up only the most distinguished literary associations. Scarcely a review was written of Wharton, Anderson, or Dreiser that did not make comparisons and contrasts with Sinclair Lewis, although Dreiser was also frequently used toward the end of the decade as a standard by which to measure the worth of Edith Wharton and Sherwood Anderson.

Of the four, Edith Wharton had been the first, strictly speaking, to be

[17] Sixten Belfrage, "En stor amerikansk författarinna," *Göteborgs-Posten*, May 21, 1932. The same implications of Cather's importance were present in Anna Lenah Elgström, "Betydande amerikansk författarinna," *Soc. Dem.*, November 16, 1936, and were repeated along with uniformly favorable comments on Cather's artistry in all later reviews of her books.

translated—her stories in *The Descent of Man and Other Stories* had appeared in 1905—but the book had been totally forgotten by the 'twenties, and it is from the appearance of *The House of Mirth* in 1922 that the real beginnings of her career in Sweden must be reckoned. In effect, therefore, Lewis preceded Edith Wharton by one year with *Main Street* in 1921; Dreiser was third with *An American Tragedy* in 1927; and finally, Anderson's *Tar* and *Dark Laughter* were translated in 1928. Lewis's prior claim upon critics and public by the circumstance of early translation was not an inconsiderable advantage, for his success was so marked from the very beginning that by virtue of his popularity he became the natural point of departure for subsequent criticism. His books, everyone had agreed, provided authentic insights into the American character and American society of a sort that had been anticipated by an imposing number of Swedish writers before him; Lewis's readers thus had come to him well prepared to seek what he had to offer. Primarily matter rather than manner, therefore, had initiated and was sustaining his critical and popular success in Sweden. So it was also with Wharton, Dreiser, and Anderson. To represent the "best" and the most "modern" in American literature, they too must inveigh against the banality of American life and furnish, if possible, an authoritative probing of the American character of the kind that was delighting Swedish readers of Lewis's books. Consequently, the standards by which Wharton, Dreiser, and Anderson were read and criticized varied very little from one to the other, and it became, for this reason, a critical convention to compare all three with Lewis, almost as though he were the master, they the disciples. The result was, of course, that some of the chief distinctions between these writers were minimized and that great stress was placed on their individual treatment of what seemed to be the great and almost sole "modern" American theme.

Only two of Sherwood Anderson's books, *Dark Laughter* and *Tar*, were translated, both in 1928, but they were given long reviews by major critics, who made frequent comparisons with Dreiser and Lewis. Although it was said that Anderson had not so much to offer as the other two and was not so good a writer, he was clearly to be named with them, for he too was engaged in social protest and rebellion against the traditional picture of America as a land of golden opportunity and high idealism. Early in the year, Dr. Österling wrote a long article on Anderson that contained the chief ingredients of ensuing criticism. Anderson is an author, Dr. Österling wrote, "not altogether like any other we know," despite some resemblances to the young Hamsun:

[He] stands in the foremost rank of novelists who during the course of the last fifteen years have revitalized American literature and have uncovered the true, unadorned face of American life. He is not as finished an author as Dreiser or Lewis; even at the age of fifty he appears to be a seeker, a wanderer still on the way, who is probing his way forward, trying many doors, and his temperament not yet fully in control. But it is precisely this fumbling that makes him interesting. He expresses the dazed restlessness of the nation, the break-through of new irresistible feelings and instincts of the soul of a people still adolescent.... Seen against the background of the massive, more or less cinema-like [narrative art of] Zolaism, Sherwood Anderson's stories may seem like shadow-play of grotesqueries and fragments. He is concerned with the same problems as other American social critics, but he perceives them differently. He prefers to portray the common man waking to consciousness— the first fluttering attempts of their souls to lift themselves over the prison wall, the agonizingly arduous processes by which the creature of habit comes to a knowledge of life's elusive beauty, and their disappointment when they find it is not enough to fill that need.[18]

Anderson's protest, Österling continued, is not intellectual and is not a product of formulas, but is made up of thoughts and memories and perceptions that cannot be synthesized into an axiom. His rebellion is mystical, and "his outburst is a confession of the homelessness of the American race." This same emphasis on the inner, non-intellectual compulsion said to have driven Anderson into authorship was repeated a few months later in another major essay. Here *Dark Laughter* was called Anderson's "artistic triumph": "A song of praise to healthy senses, to life that is larger than theory—this is no longer the gloomy psychoanalyst [of the earlier books], but the liberated poet, full of his hymn to the Ohio, the great river, childhood's great river...."[19] It is, the critic concluded, the American version of Knut Hamsun's *Pan*. Two months later still a third critic, the philosopher John Landquist, compared Anderson with Hamsun: "He recalls him in temperament, in purpose, and in the course of his life. He arouses memories of him in the admixture of poetry and irony, in the capriciousness of the impulses of thought and feeling, in his worship of vital power, in his criticism of metropolitan civilization."[20] But, he continued, Anderson's achievement does not equal Hamsun's in creative power,

[18] Anders Österling, "Sherwood Anderson," *SvD*, March 25, 1928 (and under the same title in the author's *Dagens gärning, tredje samlingen*, Stockholm, 1931, pp. 108—118).

[19] Carl-August Bolander, "Sherwood Anderson," *DN*, June 7 and 8, 1928 (and under the same title in the author's *Ismer och dikt*, Stockholm, 1928, pp. 125—136).

[20] John Landquist, "Sherwood Anderson," *Aftonbladet*, August 5, 1928.

probably because he does not have a sure enough foothold in his own milieu. Like the critics before him, Landquist was restrained from calling Anderson "the greatest" of contemporary American authors, but he is "the most immediate and perhaps the healthiest.... He preaches the value of instinct, of dreams, of the whole rich perception of life in contrast to the withering American existence and the pursuit of money, which yield nothing vital; he praises feelings as against technology, quality in life rather than quantity." Other reviews similarly praised Anderson for his courageous stand against American standardization and dwelled upon the symbolism of the river and the "dark laughter" for the primitive, unconscious, irrational, and necessary element of man's being that sooner or later, it was averred, must find release in America.[21]

One of the most interesting of the reviews of Anderson's *Dark Laughter* made no mention of his "social criticism" or rebellion against authority and was therefore refreshingly unique. "It seems," the reviewer stated,

as though Sherwood Anderson's philosophy of life could be encompassed in the words: "It is as it is." Both as a logical identity and as a moral axiom it is a principle of immobility which neutralizes the power in thought and in life. It is doubly without consolation, for the many forms of existence are thereby limited to an eternal monotony. The symbol for this conception is the great river on which boats and barges glide between factories, towns and cities, where men drudge for bread and are driven by the bustle of work and the desire for pleasure, the whole a meaningless circular course and an expression of *incapacity*, in which one of the author's mouthpieces sees all the attributes of activity. The most valuable thing in Sherwood Anderson's art is the way in which he unites milieu with consciousness ... it must be admitted that the American writer has given [this basic form of modern writing] a new shading, in which a muffled indifference, a flat repugnance is absorbed in the heavy, gray air. In this lackluster realism there is not a spark of poetry.[22]

[21] Artur Lundkvist, "Mörkt skratt," *Arbetaren*, June 20, 1928; H[enning] S[öderhiel]m, "En amerikansk roman," *GHT*, July 6, 1928; Hjalmar Gullberg, "Amerikansk och fransk exotism," *SDS*, June 18, 1928; [Anna Lenah Elgström,] "Tre gula," *Soc. Dem.*, September 18, 1928. One review, expressing great admiration for Upton Sinclair, took exception to Dr. Österling and others in their claim that Anderson presents the "unadorned face of American life," for, it was explained, Anderson, unlike Sinclair, says not one word about unemployment, class conflicts, and other capitalistic evils ("P. Fr.," "'Mörkt skratt,'" *Folkets Dagblad*, June 9, 1928).

Although never again translated, Anderson's work was occasionally reported from the American original. Carl-August Bolander reviewed *Perhaps Women* and *Hello Towns* in *Dagens Nyheter* in 1931 and found them disappointing in their uncritical view and acceptance of America.

[22] Olof Rabenius, "Amerikanskt," *ST*, June 16, 1928.

Edith Wharton's career, as it has already been said, really began in Sweden with *The House of Mirth* in 1922. Described as "at times a little diffuse and garrulous" but with a "definite excellence in its deliberate and clear-eyed method of describing, sharply but discreetly, life as it is lived at the top of the pile,"[23] this novel, like her first book in 1905, might also have been lost in the welter of genteel novels that American "lady-scribblers" (as Hamsun called them) were notorious for, had it not been partially rescued by the serious attention given all American literature in the next few years, with the result that *The House of Mirth* was occasionally recalled when the time came, in 1929, to review *Twilight Sleep*. Several other novels had been translated in the meantime, but *Twilight Sleep* was the first of Edith Wharton's books to be widely reviewed by the leading critics and the only one, probably as a consequence, to run into more than one edition. The critics agreed with Dr. Österling's comparison, in the preface to the translation, of Mrs. Manford with Babbitt; as Professor Böök said in a two-part review which he wrote of the novel, although Mrs. Manford does not have Babbitt's crude vulgarity, intellectually and morally nothing separates them, and together they give "an overpowering view of the sameness of American civilization."[24] There was repeated emphasis on Mrs. Manford's typicalness as one of the privileged rich of American society; she is

> the prototype of those ladies met by the thousands over there, elegant, richly bejeweled, carefully painted, and youthful in spirit in spite of gray hair. They seem to be made of something between iron plate and gutta percha, so indefatigable and unbending are they, but also so strangely mechanical, with an energetic "society smile" smiling away all bad things, all sorrows, and all the world's unpleasantness.[25]

Mrs. Manford, in brief, gave further proof, though in a different and smaller segment of society, of the truth of Sinclair Lewis's criticism of America. She was the female counterpart in high society of Babbitt, and the critics made of her just as great a scapegoat for the wrongs and deficiencies of American culture as they had of Babbitt. Böök was convinced that Edith Wharton was essentially European, like Mrs. Manford's daughter Nona, who "is bitter, melancholy, skeptical—in the midst of this spectacle of high society she has experienced in her quiet way something completely

---

[23] Marika Stjernstedt, "Societetstragedi," *SvD*, June 3, 1921.
[24] Fredrik Böök, "Typen Pauline Manford," *SvD*, November 11, 1929.
[25] Anna Lenah Elgström, "Edith Wharton," *Soc. Dem.*, December 23, 1929.

un-American: tragedy. She doesn't fit in; she is, in a word, European. In this respect she resembles the author of the novel."[26] Later criticism took the same view, finding in it the only explanation for Mrs. Wharton's insight into the follies of American manners and morals; in 1931 a review of *The Children,* for example, stated that Mrs. Wharton's view is limited to one small segment of society,

> but through her thorough knowledge of the American upper class, its habits and ideas, through her restrained psychological realism, which discloses the truth without surrendering to sensationalism, and through her moderately toned social satire, which is largely directed at plutocracy and social parasites, Edith Wharton has made a contribution to modern literature whose significance can be challenged neither because of the author's age nor the technique which as a child of her generation she uses. Of American authors now living there is perhaps none who has so assimilated European literary tradition as has Mrs. Edith Wharton. . . . For [she] is nearly as much French as American.[27]

And this may also be said to sum up the final Swedish impression of Edith Wharton. Although highly favorable, it came too late and could be too much qualified to offer serious competition to Lewis or Dreiser in Sweden.

Dreiser's first book to be translated into Swedish, *An American Tragedy,* did not appear until 1927, only two years before Edith Wharton's *Twilight Sleep* found favor with Swedish critics, but the monumental quality of the work and the implications for Swedish critics of its theme of tragedy in America instantly established a critical reputation in Sweden surpassing all others except Lewis's. Lewis and Dreiser—these two were regarded as the masterminds of modern American literature. Dreiser no less than Lewis, with whom he was invariably coupled in the reviews, was acclaimed as a pioneer in the heroic struggle to speak a word of truth in the land of hypocrisy and materialism. To take one example of many, a page-and-a-half article on Dreiser's America, his life, and his books explained how "the survival of the fittest" is the formula for American morality in business and industry and how "superficial idealism—excessively demonstrated to us in the average American book, film, and play—the soul's hopelessness in time of hardship, which a dependence upon external things engenders —these are the real and true American tragedies."[28] For this critic and

---

[26] Fredrik Böök, "Edith Whartons roman," *SvD*, November 18, 1929.

[27] T[orsten] F[ogelkvis]t, "Amerikansk sedesath," *DN*, November 6, 1931.

[28] Anna Lenah Elgström, "Theodore Dreiser," *Soc. Dem.,* December 4, 1927.

others Clyde Griffiths' story was a definitive study of the workings of that formula. "Life in the courts of the American temples to Mammon is narrated with a clearness and an objectivity that could not be more complete, and the downfall of an ordinary person in the tumult of a modern metropolis cannot be described with greater faithfulness."[29] In a two-part review of *An American Tragedy* and its backgrounds, Professor Böök agreed that it presents "a gigantic panorama of American life," and after noting with satisfaction that it was none other than German blood that flowed in the author's veins, he explained that the rebellion led by Dreiser and others in America against American ideals, standards, and concepts, and the whole spirit of intense discontent and embittered dissatisfaction expressed in the new literature come from an immigrant strain that has not yet been assimilated: "they have not yet been leavened by American chauvinism, which of all types is said to be the most virulent."[30] Even more Hamsunesque in his welcome of Dreiser's novel was the young literary insurgent and critic Artur Lundkvist, who in his kinship with literary rebels everywhere came to espouse the cause of American literature as his own. Dreiser, he wrote, "stands in opposition and is a radical, one of those who fight against Americanization, soul-lessness, crass materialism, moral and religious cant—the voice of one crying out among the contented and self-idolizing Philistines of 'God's own country.'"[31] Without exception[32] the critics saw that in *An American Tragedy* America was having once more a deserved rebuke of the sort that Europe had long awaited.

Discussion of the novel's style and method led invariably to contrasts with Sinclair Lewis. Dreiser's novel was called by one critic a "work of genius" that tells, as no other work has, of the tragedy of a life in the United States; even the best books by Sinclair Lewis, he declared, seem in comparison "a clear and cheerful little rill; 'An American Tragedy' is a whole river."[33] Another wrote: "He is nothing of the spirited artist, has

[29] Knut Hagberg, "En amerikansk tragedi," *NDA*, October 8, 1927.

[30] Fredrik Böök, "Det amerikanska kulturproblemet," *SvD*, October 10, 1927, and "En amerikansk tragedi," *ibid.*, October 11, 1927 (and both under the title "Theodore Dreiser" in the author's *Från fyra sekler*, Stockholm, 1928, pp. 245–263).

[31] Artur Lundkvist, "En livstragedi i det moderna Amerika," *Arbetaren*, November 1, 1927.

[32] Not until the translation of *Sister Carrie* in the following year did a critic dissent from this view; O[lle] H[olmber]g, "Tomheten," *DN*, September 23, 1928, complained that the critics had misrepresented Dreiser's novel to their Swedish readers, that Dreiser intends rather than his characters could live anywhere, for they are modern types.

[33] Knut Hagberg, "En amerikansk tragedi," *op. cit.*

nothing in him of sprightly playfulness (as does, for example, his younger colleague, Sinclair Lewis)."[34] The absence in Dreiser's writing of the "humor and irony" of *Babbitt* and Lewis's other novels became a standard observation in reviews of succeeding translations of Dreiser's books; a critic of *The Financier,* for example, wondered "what kind of book a Sinclair Lewis would have written about the same hero, how his caustic satire would have spat and hissed."[35] Although never explicitly complained of, the dissimilarity in tone and method between the two authors was never put forward as altogether to Dreiser's advantage, for once having made the observation, the critics felt compelled to plunge at once into an explanation or justification of Dreiser's style.

Dreiser's prose could be sympathetically described as "quiet, taciturn, melancholy,"[36] but much more often it was bluntly declared to be heavy, formless, and colorless—qualities that were not regarded as especially praiseworthy yet understandable and even commendable as a necessary consequence of his thorough-going naturalism. If at times his style seemed awkward, unartistic, or downright clumsy, it also was the vehicle by which an epic patience had built, sentence by sentence, an impregnable study in tragedy that despite the intellectual limitations of Dreiser's naturalism, would endure, it was said, because of his "deep pathos" and his unlimited sympathy for the lives he portrayed. "From a theoretical point of view," Professor Böök wrote,

> it is not hard to take exception to *An American Tragedy,* but it is impossible to read it without being moved and shaken, it is so full of reality, so convincing, so imaginative in its very artlessness. It tells about a weakling, but not a trace of sentimentality can be found in the presentation of his life, and willy-nilly we become deeply interested in his fate. And when we have finished the book we have got a gigantic panorama of American life as we have felt it swarming all about us. There is an endless number of facts, each as coarsely chiseled and formless as bricks; but together they build an imposing structure. Theodore Dreiser is no artist of form; his style is gray, colorless, wordy; but he is undeniably a master builder.[37]

The matter was stated perhaps most concisely early in 1930 in a review of the London edition of *A Gallery of Women:*

[34] Artur Lundkvist, "En livstragedi i det moderna Amerika," *op. cit.*
[35] Carl-August Bolander, "'Romanens Hindenburg,'" *DN,* September 28, 1929.
[36] Artur Lundkvist, "Dreiser looks at New York," *Fönstret,* No. 17 (August 23, 1930), p. 7.
[37] Fredrik Böök, "En amerikansk tragedi," *op. cit.*

He derives his artistic worth and his occasionally deeply moving pathos from a profound sympathy with the poor defenseless victims of the game [of life] and from a fatalistic belief in the destiny which rules the game and makes of individual lives a tragic-comic story, pitiful in all its pettiness but at the same time prodigious as a manifestation of faith in life and the will to live.[38]

From the first review of *An American Tragedy* to the last of *The Bulwark* in 1947, Dreiser's naturalism, though recognized at once as a literary attitude legitimatized by some of the greatest modern writers of Europe, was looked upon as a mixed blessing, for at the same time that it led to "objective veracity" and what was regarded as a salutary absence of poetic fancy, it also left Dreiser so uncritical as to be naive. This was, indeed, the nature of the "theoretical exception" that Böök had said might be taken to *An American Tragedy:*

What is characteristic of his work is its calm, objective veracity. As a thinker he is of little consequence, and the ideas which seem to emerge from his book would scarcely bear examination. His naturalism is very uncritical; evidently he embraces a kind of physiological determinism. . . . It is possible that he considers Clyde Griffiths to be a fully normal individual, a natural and irresponsible product of environment and outside influences, but that has nevertheless not prevented him from portraying his fate so truly and so rightly that the moral defects may be overlooked by the reader.[39]

This was in effect the consensus, with variations, of all leading critics. Henning Söderhielm, the Göteborg critic who continued to review Dreiser's books long after translation of them into Swedish had subsided, criticized in every review Dreiser's limitations as a thinker, but his remarks were always substantially those he had made with respect to *An American Tragedy;* behind the tragedy of Clyde Griffiths' life, he wrote, is Dreiser's picture of American life today:

It is drawn in a thousand tiny strokes, sharp and certain, but with hardly any other intention than to reproduce reality as faithfully as possible. The picture is altogether free of humor and irony and is thereby so opposed to Sinclair Lewis's method that all comparative evaluations are for the most part impossible. . . . Dreiser's relationship to the events about him seems quite unclear. He has no liking for the life that is lived in America; he is without doubt aware that it is empty, stupid, and lacking substance; but at the same time he is a fatalist, obviously convinced that the community as well as the people in

[38] H[enning] S[öderhiel]m, "Amerikanska kvinnoprofiler," *GHT,* April 29, 1930.
[39] Fredrik Böök, "En amerikansk tragedi," *op. cit.*

it merely follow nature's blind, mechanical laws and things can be no different from what they are. . . .

This fatalism, with its somewhat biological overtones, is both Dreiser's strength and his weakness. It lends monumentality to Clyde Griffiths' miserable little tragedy, for it makes of him merely a weak instrument in the hands of a pitiless fate. Clyde has no choice, and it is with a shudder of fright that the reader watches Dreiser lead his hero forward on the prescribed path. . . . It must be this way, such is life, such is man—is what the author seems to be saying. But when Dreiser embarks upon explanation for this inexorableness, only confusion results. . . .

Theodore Dreiser is not a social critic or social reformer. He is anything but a thinker or philosopher. But his naive and ungainly art achieves a rare contact with reality, and he is capable of giving intense impressions of people's lives, so that they take shape entirely free of poetic coloration. His own meditations are altogether insignificant, but what he describes compels the reader to reflections upon life such as it is and upon people such as they are. In this way, in spite of everything, he is a master.[40]

One aspect of such comments upon Dreiser's "strength and weakness" was a difference of opinion among some critics as to the credibility of his presentation of the central incident in the novel. One critic felt that regardless of Dreiser's attempts at scientific accuracy in relating the circumstances of Roberta's drowning, he had disregarded that undeniable force in human affairs called free will, which "all the psychoanalysts in the world cannot explain away."[41] Dreiser's naturalism, he complained, is so one-sided as to make the incident unconvincing. On the other hand, other critics had nothing but praise for the adroitness with which the details of the drowning were presented, and one went so far as to devote the major part of his review to commendation of Dreiser's acute insight into the psychology of crime, second only, he declared, to Dostoyevsky's.[42] Mention of resemblances to Dostoyevsky in this and other respects, however, prompted a critic of *An American Tragedy* and *Sister Carrie* in the following year to argue that the Russian would have examined his people more carefully, taken them apart, weighed them, measured them, and before he was through, made of them saints or geniuses: "For every person, even

[40] H[enning] S[öderhiel]m, "En amerikansk roman," *GHT*, November 4, 1927.

[41] Knut Hagberg, "En amerikansk tragedi," *op. cit.* Hagberg's criticism of the "one weakness" in *An American Tragedy* is of a piece, of course, with his attack on *Elmer Gantry* (see Chapter III, p. 58).

[42] Sten Selander, "Ett stycke av Amerikas själ," *Stockholms Dagblad,* November 2, 1927.

the most commonplace, is nevertheless of the same species as the saint and the genius. That was Dostoyevsky's view. According to Dreiser, every person is of the same kind as the mushroom in the soil, the machine in the shop, the phonograph record in the salon, or at his best, a well tailored, covetous animal in heat."[43]

It was agreed therefore, although for different reasons, that as a man of ideas Dreiser was of considerably less stature than Dreiser the maker of novels. A critic like Knut Hagberg, steeped in conventional ideas of morality and almost stodgily conservative, was troubled by Dreiser's implicit denial of free will; a humanistic conservative like Fredrik Böök, though not pulled into a defense of the Christian doctrine of free will, agreed substantially with Hagberg's objection when he complained of Dreiser's "physiological determinism" that made of Clyde a moral weakling, although he was portrayed as though he were completely normal; a liberal like Henning Söderhielm could find fault with the naïvetés and banalities of Dreiser's explanations of the workings of the fate, at the same time recognizing that out of Dreiser's brooding, whether naive or not, came his tragic sense; a class-conscious critic of the Communist *Ny Dag* could grumble that Dreiser was too objective and ignored the class struggle and the possibility of reform.[44] In spite of the fact that as a result of such criticism Dreiser was said to be neither a philosopher nor a thinker nor a social critic nor a psychologist nor a reformer, everyone agreed that *An American Tragedy* was the work of genius and that all his writings represented literary workmanship of the highest rank. His style was clumsy, it was everywhere said, and lacked the finely wrought quality of great art, but the painstaking accretion of minutiae to illustrate a theme inherently great gave an "epic" or "monumental" quality to his writing that would make it last. Most important for all critics was Dreiser's large, warm sympathy for his fellow men and their struggle to keep going in a cruel, inscrutable world. Whatever his defects, his love of people and his sense of personal suffering for their sorrows, coupled with his ability to tell their story without lapsing into sentimentality, were clearly the marks of

[43] O[lle] H[olmber]g, "Tomheten," *op. cit.*

[44] "En ny Dreiser," *Ny Dag*, December 3, 1930: "Dreiser believes man is driven by unknown forces. Life can be cruel, deceptive, unpleasant—this he shows in detail, but he regards that as a fact to be accepted; he never discusses the possibility of change, he does not see the economic development of society, the movement of the masses, the class struggle, but merely individuals." Other critics, not of the Communist persuasion, complained frequently of Dreiser's dealing with types rather than individuals.

a great tragic artist. Dr. Österling, a dissenting member of the committee that awarded the Nobel Prize to Sinclair Lewis, summed up all this in 1931 by asking: "Is he a materialist or an idealist? He can be the one as much as the other, but most constant is an extraordinary fascination for him of human existence." At one point, he continued, Dreiser says the world lives by illusions which quickly disappear upon inspection; at another, he feels certain there must be some higher intelligence which treats men like playthings. "Between these poles all of Dreiser's philosophy lies, so remarkably uncertain in comparison with his ability to give immediacy to his descriptions of people, scenes, and events."[45]

The publication record of translations of Dreiser, coming as they did in successive years, looks better than it actually was: *An American Tragedy* (1927), *Sister Carrie* (1928), *The Financier* (1929), *Jennie Gerhardt* (1930), and *The Titan* (1930). Except for *The "Genius"* in 1936, nothing else was translated until *The Bulwark* in 1947. *An American Tragedy* was the most highly esteemed by critics and had the best sales; nearly half of the edition of 4,000 copies was sold soon after it appeared in the stores, whereas only some 750 copies (of an edition of 4,000) of *Sister Carrie* had immediate sale, and about 460 copies (of 3,000) of *The Financier,* the record also of *Jennie Gerhardt* and *The Titan.* Only the sales of *An American Tragedy* could match those of Sinclair Lewis's books, which by the mid-twenties could be expected to have an immediate sale of at least a thousand copies, a few so far exceeding that figure as to require second editions within a year or two.[46]

When *Sister Carrie* was translated in 1928, Dr. Österling observed, "It is a strange fact that the new American literature has won a foothold in Europe chiefly through its group of social critics and rebels—Sinclair Lewis, Theodore Dreiser, and Sherwood Anderson."[47] The attention given Edith Wharton's *Twilight Sleep* in the following year would certainly have warranted the addition of her name to the list, so that by 1930 the case for modern American literature rested chiefly in Sweden with these four writers, each of them capable in his own way of giving Swedish readers confirmation of the traditional concept of America consigned to them by Hamsun and the Swedish writers that came after him, and each of them acclaimed in the first place for that reason alone. As admirable as the

[45] Anders Österling, "Dreisers läroår," *SvD,* August 22, 1931.

[46] Publication figures through the courtesy of Mr. Bengt Petri and Miss Karin Marcus of Norstedt & Söner.

[47] Anders Österling, "Amerikanskt genomsnitt," *SvD,* October 4, 1928.

work of such writers as Upton Sinclair, Joseph Hergesheimer, Willa Cather, and even Ellen Glasgow could occasionally be, they either did not sustain their criticism of America in the expected manner, or did it weakly, or not at all, and they were accordingly assigned minor parts in what the critics felt was the only American literature of importance. Indeed, Dr. Österling's intimation that there was another kind or that other equally promising writers did exist is the only such comment of the time that has come to hand. Writers usually associated with the 'twenties in America either were not translated or were effectively ignored until the following decade or even later in Sweden. Hemingway, it is true, was first translated in 1929 but did not gain general critical acceptance and popularity until the 'forties; Dos Passos was not translated until 1931; Fitzgerald's *The Great Gatsby* appeared in 1928 but was completely disregarded until reprinted in the late 'forties; Bromfield's promising early career did not make itself felt in Sweden until the late 'thirties; Faulkner was not translated until 1944. Occasionally the critics took quick glances at such popular writers in the 'twenties as Kathleen Norris and Edna Ferber. They were just as quickly dismissed as "unimportant" primarily because there could be little doubt of their not belonging to "the social critics and rebels" or because their protest—as Ruben Berg said of Edna Ferber, for example— was "pleasantly seasoned" in order to make the truth about America more palatable, less apparent, and less disturbing.[48]

The persistence of Swedish criticism of American books in the 'twenties in cultivating only those authors who could meet the crucial test of attacking what had been viewed from Hamsun's time on as the gravest deficiencies of American character and culture, may have led to blind spots in summarily dividing American writers into two camps, the philistines (like Booth Tarkington and Kathleen Norris) and the rebels (like Michael Gold and Floyd Dell as well as Sinclair Lewis and Theodore Dreiser), with the result that every book was examined first as a social document or battle communiqué from the one warring faction or the other, and only second as literature; but the taking of sides—rather, the giving of sides— gave criticism an urgency, even a militancy, that it probably would not have otherwise had, and the writers that benefited by it benefited handsomely. The narrowness of the focus gave intensity to the scrutiny and turned a burning light on one of the most controversial subjects of the day—America. Toward the end of the decade more thoughtful critics

---

[48] Ruben Berg, "En ny amerikansk författarinna," *Aftonbladet,* December 6, 1925.

gradually grew either wary or weary of facilely bandying about the symbol that "Babbitt" had become, and novels were not so readily ticketed as pro- or anti-Babbitt as before, but it took another generation—that of the 'thirties and 'forties—to get rid of the oversimplifications of the dichotomy and get back to first principles of literary criticism. Before criticism could advance, however, the resistance from pre-war days to American literature had to be very much lowered, a break-through had to be made. Paradoxically, it was done almost wholly in terms of the criticism of Hamsun and Hallström and Berger and others, those who had in the first place built up the resistance to American literature and the scorn for American culture. The conventional concept of American culture given by these critics to a people virtually totally ignorant of that culture made them highly receptive, as we have seen, to the American writers who seemed to confirm those long-held views.

CHAPTER V

The Award of the Nobel Prize to Sinclair Lewis

Apart from directions as to who may propose candidates for the Nobel Prize, the sole stipulation in Alfred Nobel's will of 1895 concerning the annual prize in literature is that it be given to the person producing "the most distinguished work of an idealistic tendency." The task of choosing from among candidates proposed by members of the Swedish, French and Spanish Academies or similar institutions and by university teachers of esthetics, literature, and history, is entrusted to a committe of three poets, novelists, or playwrights who are members of the Swedish Academy. In 1930 the Nobel Committee was made up of Erik Axel Karlfeldt, whose poetry has become one of the classics of modern Swedish literature and who was himself awarded the Nobel Prize posthumously in 1931; Per Hallström, a member of the Academy since 1908, whose disappointment in America has already been noted; and the poet Anders Österling, a member of the Academy since 1919 and its permanent secretary since 1941. The proceedings of the Nobel Committee are kept strictly from public view, but not infrequently enough is known of the candidacies to arouse speculation and debate privately and sometimes even in the press. Such was particularly true of the Committee's deliberations in 1930, when it was common knowledge that an American author was to be chosen, and indeed that the choice lay toward the last between Lewis and Dreiser.

Why an American? Only once before—in 1913 when Rabindranath Tagore was awarded the prize—had the Committee gone outside continental Europe, Scandinavia, and the British Isles for its award of the prize; from 1901, when Sully-Prudhomme became the recipient of the first award of the prize in literature, to 1930 the prize had been conferred fully or in equal shares eighteen times upon continental Europeans (most frequently Frenchmen and Germans, and never a Russian), seven times upon Scandinavians, twice upon Irishmen, once upon an Englishman, and once, as we have already said, upon an Indian. Whether by necessity or intent, therefore, the tradition was principally Western European. It also was strongly conservative in the frequent choice of recipients whose writing careers were essentially completed at the time of the award, for more than half had been over sixty years of age. The award to Lewis was unusual because he was an American and presumably, therefore, unable to draw upon the traditional resources of the great European *kulturländer* or even the ancient wisdom of the East. It was also unusual because of his youth: only Rudyard Kipling, who received the award in 1907 at the age of forty-two, had been younger. At forty-five, Lewis showed promise of further achievement. Moreover, Dr. Österling has stated[1] that the award to Lewis was also unique in having been made in the first year the candidate was presented to the Committee. There is no question, therefore, that the Committee had compelling reasons for choosing an American even when that meant deciding between two relatively young men (Dreiser was not yet fifty in 1930) in the first year of their candidacies. We have to seek no further for the most cogent reason for the choice of an American than to recall the lively activity in translation and criticism during the decade—a reflection, to be sure, of the great upsurge of general interest in all aspects of American life and culture, but also a sure sign of a deepening admiration in Sweden of American literature. By 1930 one could no longer doubt that this was a thriving literature of permanent value. It was, however, a literature whose chief representatives were speaking what Swedes had long suspected to be the truth about America. And in saying so much, we are also saying that the criteria by which American literature was being judged excellent were not in the first place literary but sociological, for they were derived from extra-literary critical views of America expressed by Hamsun, Hallström, Berger, and others. American literature in the 1920's was primarily interesting to the Swedes as social document which brilliantly justified European superiority over New World culture. This approach to American literature determined the course of the critical reception of it in Sweden and was therefore responsible, paradoxically, for the high position given to American literature at the end of the decade. A brief review of the Swedish reading of American literature in the 'twenties will show why this was so and also why the particular choice for the Nobel Prize was Sinclair Lewis.

We have seen how at the beginning of the decade the Swedish attitude toward America still bore the impress of the arrogant, satirical criticism of America by Knut Hamsun in 1889; it was highly subjective criticism,

[1] In conversation with the present writer, March 3, 1950.

superficial in its observations and hopelessly entangled in the turbulent personality of its author. Somewhat milder yet equally subjective, in spite of their efforts to give it the detachment of art in short stories and novels, was the reaction to America expressed by the Swedes Per Hallström, Henning Berger, and Gustaf Hellström. Similar views were occasionally expressed by other Swedish writers, from such a minor poet as Sigurd Agrell to Hjalmar Söderberg, Hjalmar Bergman, and Erik Axel Karlfeldt. Whatever form the criticism took and however much or little of it may have occupied the thinking of these writers, the reaction was essentially the same: alarm at the threatening spread of a tyranny of mediocrity engendered in an irresponsible, traditionless democracy and nurtured in the forcing-bed of American materialism and pragmatism. No wonder, then, that a common epithet for America was jungle—an untended, carelessly abundant land full of tricks and pitfalls for the unwary but smugly said by its natives to be "the garden spot of the world." The Americans' blithe unawareness of their faults and their failure to recognize that they existed in a cultural vacuum disturbed these critics so much that it became an axiom among them, accepted apparently without question by their readers, that of a land in such dire straits nothing but cultural aridity could be expected. The conviction was, if anything, strengthened by the sensational Jack London vogue and the lesser popularity of Upton Sinclair, whose appeal was chiefly to a group of readers and writers as yet unrecognized in Swedish literature.

A Swedish public brought at last by the results of World War I to the necessity to learn about American civilization seized gladly upon American writers just then emerging whose strictures upon America were recognizable or could be interpreted into recognizability. Lewis had been the first in Sweden and most conspicuous in both America and Sweden in castigating America. His outcry in *Main Street* reverberated throughout America and placed the Swedes in a new listening posture; when *Babbitt* appeared they were more than ready for it. Here was the book that spectacularly corroborated everything that had been said about America from Hamsun's time on; the "doubter" that Hamsun had believed could not emerge in uncritical America had now appeared in the person of Sinclair Lewis. In this vein Lewis was welcomed, and for this reason he left in Sweden an indelible impression of not only his own perspicacity and shrewdness but of the necessary form of American literature to come. Each important new author appearing in translation had first to pass the test of being a "true spirit" in rebellion before other qualities in his writing could be properly appreciated. In this frame of mind, and taking cues now from such critics as Stuart Sherman, Van Wyck Brooks, Régis Michaud, and particularly H. L. Mencken, to all of whom reference was increasingly made as the decade wore on, the critics, aided of course by publishers prompt to capitalize on Lewis's popularity by offering similar wares, praised such writers as Edith Wharton, Sherwood Anderson, and Theodore Dreiser (to mention only those who were reckoned among Lewis's peers) for their contribution to the stirring and long overdue protest against American cultural, social, and even physical shortcomings. As several as their approaches to the problem were, these writers had that intent of social satire in common and their importance (rather than their intrinsic literary worth) was measured primarily according to their success as critics of America. Their achievement in turn accrued to Lewis's advantage in thereby strengthening his reputation as a courageous pioneer and minor prophet: he had been the first and he had continued his work undaunted by adversities. As a consequence, his best book, *Babbitt*—fondly regarded as a remarkably felicitous combination of the most attractive American trait, good humor, and the rarest, self-criticism—had made so lasting an impression that all else was judged by it, and all else, with the possible exception of *An American Tragedy,* was found wanting. Thus, because of the necessity imposed upon Sweden after World War I to take cognizance of the new world power in the west, it came about that a country virtually ignorant of American culture before 1920 and possessed of a body of prejudices in spirit closely allied to the sweeping animadversions of a Mrs. Trollope or a Lepel Griffin of forty or more years earlier, turned in the 1920's to learn about American culture and was confirmed in its prejudices by the literature it found there. Thus, too, the author who had blazed the trail, as far as the Swedes were concerned, in advancing that literature and who was for literary reasons its chief spokesman, was rewarded at the end of the decade with the Nobel Prize.

Lewis's only rival for the prize was Dreiser, whose *An American Tragedy* had made a deep impression in 1927. As much as Edith Wharton was admired, her reputation as a serious critic of America came late—in 1929 with *Twilight Sleep*—and her concentration upon the doings of upper-class New York society was universally felt to limit her powers as a satirist. Sherwood Anderson's reputation in Sweden rested almost solely on two books translated in 1928, one of which, *Dark Laughter,* was said to have stylistic advantages over what one usually found in American fiction, but the protest against American manners and morals was blunted by an interesting but undefined and somewhat naive primitivism. And so the field was narrowed to Lewis and Dreiser. Their respective qualifications, as the Swedes judged them, were discussed in a series of articles appearing in the Stockholm paper *Dagens Nyheter* immediately prior to the announcement of the award. They were written by the critic Torsten Fogelqvist, an intimate friend of Karlfeldt, chairman of the Nobel Committee in 1930. After reporting that rumor had it that the two contenders for the prize were Dreiser and Lewis, and then duly discounting any special knowledge he might have been imputed to have to confirm or deny the rumor, Fogelqvist without further hesitation opened a general discussion of modern American literature: "One thing is certain, and that is that modern American literature, however one may judge American culture in relation to European, is neither a quantité nor a qualité négligeable, but a factor which we must reckon with in the greatest seriousness."[2] Condescension marked the remainder of his exposition of general trends in American literature, which, having no old literary traditions behind it, he explained, cannot always be distinguished from journalism. American writers of the nineteenth century wrote apart from life: Cooper and Thoreau tarrying in the woods, Emerson constructing a work of beauty in his ivory tower, Poe probing the mysteries of the soul, Mark Twain entertaining with stories of adventure, humor, and caricature, and none having anything whatever to do with the average American and his machines "who is struggling to make over the whole world to a great stone and asphalt metropolis." Even when these earlier writers tried to be realistic, he continued, they were denied success by the restraints of puritanism and romanticism, and it was not until the turn of the century, when the effects of immigration and industrialization and the kept press began to be oppressive, that the protest against the devaluation of the individual began and reaction to puritanism became a literary force strengthened by the movement in world literature called naturalism. And for this reason, he concluded, life in America— compounded of piety, its concomitant hypocrisy, and the necessary corrective to both, blasphemy—has been a richer source of literary material than that of Europe, which has rid itself of puritanical restrictions. Frank Norris he named as the first of America's modern realists; Upton Sinclair is perhaps best known in Europe, but since *The Jungle* his criticism has lost its fire; and Edgar Lee Masters, whom Fogelqvist quoted at some

[2] Torsten Fogelqvist, "Modern amerikansk realism: I. Ett inledande radioföredrag," *DN*, October 17, 1930.

length, has revealed in regionalistic poetry the hypocrisy and self-contradictions of typical Americans of the small town.

Obviously nothing in this first of five articles shows any great advance in attitude toward or knowledge about American literature since the days of Knut Hamsun: if America now has a literature worthy of the name, it is almost in spite of itself, and the best of that literature reveals the low state into which mankind has fallen in an industrialized, uncultured society. Fogelqvist's next two articles, on Dreiser, and his final two, on Lewis, were essentially elaborations of the premises of his first article, but now the advance beyond Hamsun's kind of criticism becomes evident in the careful but brief survey of the careers and principal works of both authors, which occupied most of the critic's space and fixed *An American Tragedy* and *Babbitt* as masterpieces of the new American movement in self-criticism. Comparing the two authors, he declared Lewis the probable inferior to Dreiser in the massive strength and size of the latter's picture of society and in the panoramic scope and monumentality of his work, but definitely superior temperamentally and artistically, particularly in matters of style, for Dreiser, he explained, has no trace of humor, and Lewis is a born humorist—something of a Dickens or Mark Twain. Dreiser is a satirist of society but his style is too heavy for irony, whereas Lewis swings between humor and irony, which though perhaps not lethal is full of barbs and stings. Finally, Lewis is much Dreiser's superior in catching all the overtones of the speech of his characters. Having thus determined upon Lewis, the critic summed up his achievement:

Sinclair Lewis's works are an indiscreet satire not merely of hypocrisy but equally of the standardization of the soul of man, of the involvement of heart and mind in a commercial and cheap system of ready-made wares. In a collectivistic era and milieu he has had the courage to strike a blow for the right of individual decision, responsibility, reason and personal taste, which is the natural atmosphere of free man and the breath of cultural life insofar as one understands by culture something other and more than mass production, money, comfort, and speed. One may say that his novels constitute a literary illustration of André Siegfried's economic, social, and moral observations of the United States today.... Lewis at bottom is as good an American as any. He could never have portrayed Babbitt and Dodsworth as he has done if he had not in his innermost being a strong sympathy with both.... It is their weakness that Lewis likes in his Americans: the childishness, the immaturity, their human goodness and helpfulness, their somewhat robust decency, their perplexity and precipitous bursts of passion, the naive and deep chest tones which can be set free in secret sobbing or burst out in hearty, rumbling laughter.... No, it is not the man, but the mask and the pretense which Sinclair Lewis scoffs, derides, bombards, and hates.[3]

Comments in the Swedish press before and at the time of the announcement were almost unanimously of Fogelqvist's opinion, though less concerned perhaps with extending Lewis's satire beyond the American scene. The prevailing opinion was substantiated by the official presentation speech given by Karlfeldt at the Nobel Festival on December 10, 1930. Although he too spoke of *Main Street* as one of the best descriptions ever written of a small town, whether American or European, the main thesis of his speech was that Lewis had been the first to use the satirical powers of an artist against the middleclass complacency and hypocrisy common to our civilization but taking its worst form under the name "Americanism." Of Zenith he said that it "is a hundred times as large as Gopher Prairie and therefore a hundred times richer in one-hundred-percent Americanism and one hundred times as satisfied with itself; and the enchantment of its optimism and progressive spirit is embodied in George F. Babbitt."[4] Lewis's excellence, he explained, lies first in his satire, which in *Babbitt* is a triumph of art almost unique in literature, and then in his gift for words, particularly his ability to reproduce conversation. Karlfeldt summarized the themes of *Main Street* and *Babbitt* and also of three other books, which though important were obviously not so highly regarded as the first two: *Arrowsmith,* which is sound in its medical facts and never superficial in its details; *Elmer Gantry,* in which Lewis was neither willing nor able to give his central character any attractive traits, but which as description is "a feat of strength, genuine and powerful, and its full-flavored, sombre satire has a devastating effect";[5] and *Dodsworth,* a study of the Europe–America problem by a member of the most aristocratic circle in Zenith, Sam Dodsworth.

All the circumstances of the award, from the time of its announcement to the Nobel Festival, were carefully reported by a well pleased press. Lewis was interviewed in New York before embarking, aboard the *Drottningholm* when he landed at Göteborg, on the train to Stockholm, and at the Grand

[3] Torsten Fogelqvist, "Modern amerikansk realism: III. Sinclair Lewis," *DN*, November 1, 1930.

[4] Erik Axel Karlfeldt, *Why Sinclair Lewis Got the Nobel Prize....* New York [1930], pp. 2—3.

[5] *Ibid.,* p. 7.

Hotel there; everyone was curious to know what babbittries an American author would commit, and he was asked his opinion on a wide range of subjects, from what he really thought about other American authors to his ideas about Sweden (where he had never been). But Lewis confounded and delighted his interviewers all the way with his accessibility and his almost overweening modesty, and at every opportunity he named a dozen or more authors, including Dreiser, O'Neill, Cather, Wharton, Sinclair, and an assortment of Europeans, who he insisted would have the prize if he were charged with bestowing it.[6] The press called him "the representative of the American temperament when it is best and of American literature at its most mature,"[7] and saw in the award a breakdown of the old prejudices that America is "a collection of Yankees greedy for money and sensation, without taste, education, and culture."[8] But, it was cautiously added, the fact that the Academy awarded the prize to a critic of America shows that it does not uncritically accept "all the values which this new culture wishes to endow us with." Even in this moment of beneficence the old ingrained fears could not be altogether effaced.

Lewis's Nobel address, "The American Fear of Literature,"[9] was characteristic of him—serious criticism blended with some fussing, some good-natured ribbing, and much generosity—and it was well received, although his lingering over the shortcomings of the American Academy of Arts and Letters, of American universities, and of the "New Humanism," some felt not to be altogether appropriate to the dignity of such an address and wished he had confined himself to what did in fact take up most of his speech, an open-handed naming of authors who might well have received the prize: Dreiser, who "more than any other man, marching alone, usually unappreciated, often hated, has cleared the trail from Victorian and Howellsian timidity and gentility in American fiction to honesty and boldness and passion of life";[10] O'Neill, "who has done nothing much in American drama save to transform it utterly, in ten or twelve years, from a false world of neat and competent trickery to a world of splendor and fear and

[6] "Askungen," "Mr. Lewis at home: En visit år 1929," *SvD*, November 6, 1930; "Babbitts far intervjuar mr S. Lewis," *DN*, December 9, 1930; "Sinclair Lewis anlände i natt till Göteborg," *SvD*, December 9, 1930.

[7] "Sinclair Lewis fick årets litterära nobelpris," *SvD*, November 6, 1930.

[8] T[orsten] F[ogelqvis]t, "Sinclair Lewis erhöll årets litteraturpris," *DN*, November 6, 1930.

[8] In Karlfeldt, *Why Sinclair Lewis Got the Nobel Prize . . .*, pp. 9—23.

[10] *Ibid.*, p. 13.

greatness";[11] and Cabell, Cather, Mencken, Anderson, Sinclair, Hergesheimer, and Hemingway—all of whom, had they been honored with the prize, Lewis assured his listeners, would have provoked heavy groans of disapproval from America, because of "the fact that in America most of us—not readers alone but even writers—are still afraid of any literature which is not a glorification of our faults as well as our virtues."[12] This, the central theme of the address, we may be sure rang familiarly in Swedish ears. Hadn't Hamsun said precisely this forty years before?

In reaction to the award, a classic example of criticism in the Hamsun tradition appeared in 1931 in the conservative *Ord och Bild* and was characteristically entitled "Sinclair Lewis and the Problem of America."[13] As the first article, apart from minor notices of translations, on a North American literary subject to appear since Andrea Butenschön's essay on Walt Whitman in 1905 in what was then Scandinavia's leading literary journal, it demonstrates vividly the effect of the prize upon conservative Swedish opinion; laced with the same kind of disdain, mockery, and superciliousness that we are familiar with in Hamsun's book on America, it represents at once the culmination and defeat of the trend in Swedish criticism of American culture that had predominated for so many years.

The critic began with personal reminiscences of the undignified, "music hall" atmosphere of an American Legion parade which he had seen in Paris at the end of the war. He described the contingents of "Napoleonic grenadiers, Hungarian hussars, Spanish bullfighters, cowboys from the Wild West, tennis champions with a following of cute boys and girls ... [and] a professional Indian fire-eater from Montparnasse in full dress, feathers and all," followed by "middle-aged Gibson girls in trousers with guns on their shoulders" marching by in perfect Prussian style to jazz tunes echoing between the old weathered palaces. All this had inspired a little poilu to remark: "Mais ce n'est pas sérieux tout cela, c'est de music hall!"[14] and the critic agreed heartily in this first and last personal encounter with American life. He recalled that the young Hamsun had suffered much the same reaction to flamboyant American patriotism, which is "just as limitless as it is loud-mouthed." No wonder, then, that in their standardized nation with its militant optimism Americans have so loudly protested the award of the Nobel Prize to Lewis.

[11] *Ibid.*, p. 13.   [12] *Ibid.*, p. 11.
[13] Kjell Strömberg, "Sinclair Lewis och problemet Amerika," *Ord och Bild*, XL (1931), 153—161.
[14] *Ibid.*, 153.

America has not been able to forget the lesson, or rather the overdue lesson, it got in *Main Street, Babbitt,* and *Elmer Gantry.* It will not gladly do so soon. This now so painful memory will perhaps contribute toward fewer monkey-trials à la Dayton in the future and toward dulling Mr. Chaplin's [!] eagerness to play Jesus as a cheerful and goodnatured Rotary man to the lasting benefit of the Christian religion. Perhaps America will one day actually begin more generally to doubt that prosperity and success in the form of automobiles, radios, and phonographs, in addition to unlimited access to smuggled liquor, determine human values. There are plenty naive and pushing souls in Europe who stand ready to transplant Mr. Babbitt's standardized civilization here among us, and not least in our beloved Sweden. And what is Messrs. Stalin's and Mussolini's art of statesmanship other than a bold effort to convert Moscow and Rome to glorious sisters of the good city of Zenith?

Sinclair Lewis is far from being the only, but is undoubtedly from a literary point of view the most mature of modern American authors; he has taken on the job of telling his countrymen the truth about themselves, the whole truth, armed with both antlers and teeth.[15]

Strömberg's summaries of the plots and themes of the more important novels stressed in like manner their rebellion against American life. He concluded that Lewis's criticism is essentially that of such French critics as André Siegfried, Lucien Romier, and Paul Morand:

It is gratifying to find that a typically American author, like Sinclair Lewis, reported as talented, not to say gifted with genius, shares, in one of the great and urgent cultural problems of today, the opinion which is advanced by Europe's elite, regardless of name and nationality.... The disintegration of the elite is everywhere a dangerous threat. America and Russia offer much material for study at the moment from this point of view. It seems to me that Sinclair Lewis in his literary production has significantly contributed toward facilitating conditions conducive to a higher type of man in Mr. Babbitt's standardized Utopia. He has, in other words, honestly come by the Nobel Prize.[16]

The unquestioned identification of Lewis's intent with the "European elite's" point of view, the usurpation of that point of view on the slimmest evidence, and the assumption—to get closer to the central problem of all this criticism—that Lewis's books were primarily intended as social documents of protest from which hope might be derived for America's future

[15] *Ibid.,* 154
[16] *Ibid.,* 161.

coming of age, sum up the essentials of Strömberg's criticism and of nearly all Swedish criticism of American literature up to this time.

It was to take another generation of critics and readers—and indeed another generation of American writers—before the emphasis in the interpretation of American literature shifted from this lopsided view of it as document and prophesy to a more balanced consideration of it as work of art, set perhaps in an American scene but pregnant with possibilities beyond social commentary. A sign of the change in the Swedish critical approach to this literature was already evident in Dr. Österling's dissent from the majority decision of the Nobel Committee, a difference of opinion that preferred Dreiser to Lewis but was overruled, as he has later said,[17] by Hallström's private and published admiration for Lewis, which was seconded by Karlfeldt. As we have seen, both Hallström and Karlfeldt shared the current view of America as a smug, materialistic land in need of a reverse, and both found in Lewis the American who had wittily and powerfully delivered the first blows. Österling, however, saw more permanent values in Dreiser than in Lewis, for Dreiser's books were related only incidentally to timely criticism of America. But also for Österling Dreiser's pioneering for the sake of a new literature had importance; so at least we may judge from a review of *The Bulwark* in 1947:

> In time [Dreiser] came to be regarded as the great pioneer in American literature, the stubborn and uncompromising warrior who took the worst blows and cleared the way for the younger generation. Today his foremost work, "An American Tragedy," emerges still as a monument of solid greatness and convincing power; in its vicinity there is nothing that has the same chance of lasting. When the Nobel Prize of 1930 was awarded Dreiser's younger competitor, Sinclair Lewis, there were many who felt that the older man should have had it. In retrospect it may be said without hesitation that these persons were right.[18]

Among those "who felt that the older man should have had it" was the young critic and poet Artur Lundkvist, who, to be sure, preferred James Joyce as a candidate before all others, but who nevertheless felt that since the prize was to go to an American there were others far more deserving than Lewis: Edgar Lee Masters, for instance, for his *Spoon River Anthology*, or Sherwood Anderson for his consistently high quality, or Carl Sandburg,

[17] In conversation with the present writer, March 3, 1950.
[18] Anders Österling, "Dreisers sista roman," *ST*, May 12, 1947.

"America's most genuine poet," but especially Dreiser, who "without a single doubt" excels them all:

> He has gravity and constant strength; he reaches down much deeper than Lewis does. His love of life, his seriousness, his unswerving truth and consistency cannot be outweighed by Lewis's wit, his journalistically quick and pliable style with its artistic touch, and his elegant, colorful characterization. Lewis shows a tendency to become fastened to a mannerism, to depict time after time the same Babbitt, the same Main Street. He gives little hope of renewal; in general he has apparently said all that he has to say; there may well be variations, undoubtedly arresting but scarcely of significance. To be sure, not much more can be expected either of Dreiser; he is distinctly older in years also, but his existing work contains a greater wealth, a life of greater genuineness and substance, a greater number of varied and independent characters, set in milieus depicted with extraordinary reliability and wealth of detail. Technically, Dreiser is assuredly more old-fashioned than Lewis, but this does not appear to be so important, especially when both of them employ a style that is hardly up-to-date: for that, one need only turn to Joyce.[19]

Although the critics continued to be well-disposed toward Lewis in his later books, his reputation soon declined from its high point in 1930. The Nobel award had occasioned the reprinting of four of his earlier books then out of print (*Free Air, The Job, Elmer Gantry,* and *Dodsworth*), and the efforts of one small publisher, Federativ, in obtaining rights to Lewis's *Cheap and Contented Labor* embarrassed Lewis's regular Swedish publisher when the book appeared less than a week after the announcement of the award and went immediately into two reprintings for a total of 8,000 copies. *Ann Vickers,* which appeared in 1933, appealed to public and critics alike as a renewed attack on specifically American conditions by the old master in one of his best moments, but thereafter, with *Work of Art* in 1934, *It Can't Happen Here* in 1937, *The Prodigal Parents* in 1938, *Bethel Merriday* in 1941, *Gideon Planish* in 1944, and *Kingsblood Royal* in 1949, it became increasingly common to speak of Lewis's "negative criticism" and the repetitiousness of theme and method, and to open a review with the chilling observation that "this is clearly not one of his more significant books." Most critics had obviously lost enthusiasm for Lewis's "one-sided" attack on America and nearly all were hard put to know what to say about the possible truth of his comments on theatrical conditions, prison life, philanthropy, and Naziism in America; they supposed him well-

[19] Artur Lundkvist, "Nobelpris med adress Amerika," *Fönstret,* No. 29 (November 15, 1930), p. 10.

meaning but perhaps too polemical and a little rash, and then excused these faults in the hope that his book might "do some good." But the feeling prevailed that this was an unorthodox way of criticizing a piece of literature, and reservations had to be made about Lewis's "artistry," his "profundity," and even about the soundness of his point of view, which in the 'twenties had been his most endearing quality. In 1939 Artur Lundkvist, in a little booklet surveying the work of Lewis, Dreiser, and Anderson, finished the task he had begun in 1930 in writing off Lewis:

> Does not the decline in Lewis's writing depend upon the fact that his art, which is that of reporting, has lost contact with present day reality? America in some measure has possibly grown away from him; its frailties and its absurdities are no longer exactly what they were in the immediately preceding decade. He is an author who is ultimately dependent upon temporary circumstances. He does not drive down to the permanent and the constant within man and society. He does not create figures with independent life, but deals in types, mouthpieces, and effectively simplified minor characters. He possesses no really comprehensive knowledge of life, like Dreiser, for example; and he lacks true imagination, however ingenious he may be in staging the incidents on display. His ideas are rather indefinite, and he has none of the artist's passion which would have been able to raise him above the level of current interests determined by the times.[20]

Still later, it was possible for the editor of *Dagens Nyheter* to look back on Lewis's career and say: "The 1920's were Lewis's great and happy period. Then came a string of books that are so pathetic because we see him trying to recapture his former strength; the old, brilliant characters now return distorted, diffused, impossible."[21]

Although *The "Genius"* and *The Bulwark* were the only books of Dreiser's to be translated after 1930, his critical reputation, as we have seen, grew even if he was not widely read. His style continued to trouble critics and public alike, but the thoroughness of his careful building up of details in massive studies of modern life, all ambitiously set in a comprehensive naturalistic framework, was taken as a true mark of a painstaking artist, regardless of the lapses and ineptitudes that he might be guilty of in final analysis. The London editions of *Dawn, The Color of a Great City,* and *Hey Rub-a-Dub-Dub* were reviewed in a few of the leading newspapers, and Dreiser's activities were regularly reported in the

[20] Artur Lundkvist, *Tre Amerikaner,* Stockholm, 1939 (Studentföreningen Verdandis småskrifter No. 415), pp. 44—45.

[21] Herbert Tingsten, "Sinclair Lewis' lyckliga år," *DN,* February 3, 1953.

news columns. Sherwood Anderson, for whose mysticism Lundkvist formed a very special attachment, had otherwise little interest for critics or readers after 1928; a few of his later books were reviewed (with disappointment at their apparent desertion of satire of America, which had been regarded as Anderson's forte), but none was translated. Edith Wharton was always referred to with admiration, but mention of her name became increasingly seldom after her last book was translated in 1931.

The decline of so many reputations makes it clear that the satirists of American life were now no longer the darlings of the Swedish critics, who busied themselves in recovering from the shock of Lewis and his contemporaries. Much of the force of the Hamsun line of criticism was spent by the 'thirties, and another generation of American writers was now accepted without apology by critics eager to go beyond caustic allusions to the terrors of life in America and self-congratulation on the exposure of that life by American writers. The need was now seldom if ever felt to read an American author as a representative of a remote but ever threatening way of life or to extol his merits in terms of a cultural background peculiar to himself or to a national literary movement. As Karlfeldt had hinted in his Nobel Address and as a few critics had said outright still earlier, the "problem of America"—the problem of the individual and of art in an increasingly collectivistic, industrialized, urban society— was no longer so glibly regarded as exclusively America's, nor was only America to blame for accelerating the rise of the problem all over the world. Instead, critical essays began more and more to focus their attention upon the universalities to be found in American literature, upon literary values, and particularly upon literary techniques. Whereas Lewis had had evidently no influence whatever upon Swedish writers, and Dreiser only upon one, the novelist Fritz Thorén,[22] American writers of the succeeding decades were enlisted in Swedish literary causes (that often subjected their work to special interpretation) and were even taken as models. To tell of the reception of American literature in Sweden in the 'thirties and 'forties would therefore require a study of such clear influences as well as a survey of the number and kind of translations and the criticism of them. Necessary to consider, for example, would be the adaptation of the spirit and ideas of Walt Whitman, Carl Sandburg, Sherwood Anderson, and others to the literary theories expounded by Artur Lundkvist for the important group of writers known as "de fem unga" ("the five youths"), which included

[22] Suggested by Olle Holmberg in his obituary tribute, "Fritz Thorén död," *DN*, February 16, 1950.

the major novelist and poet Harry Martinson, said also to have been influenced in early years by Jack London. Lundkvist's collection of essays, *Atlantvind* (Stockholm, 1932), supported its theme of "dynamic modernism," the guiding principle of the group in its early, formative days, by emphasizing the primitivism of American autodidacts, "self-taught men with no diplomas in their pockets, with no academic study behind them,"[23] who rejected convention in life and academic taboos in literature, whose "hunger for life" became the "worship of life" in all its modern forms. Thus he spoke of Whitman as "Manhattan's son with the broad chest of a proletarian,"[24] and of Carl Sandburg as the representative of the masses, who writes of "street workers, factory slaves, day laborers, loggers, hooligans; people from the streets and work places who talk their own rich, free, and bold speech, smell of the slums, sweat, and machine oil."[25] "Dynamic modernism" could also be discerned in the work of Sherwood Anderson, "the seeker, the dreamer, the mystic, . . . the poor boy of the Middle West, the itinerant worker,"[26] and in O'Neill, the experimenter in new forms, and in Thomas Wolfe, the rebel protesting "standardized existence" and worshiping "not the life enclosed in the confines of culture, but life as an unknown force beyond all pitiful, unsatisfying forms,"[27] and so on through a list of writers that included Eugene Jolas as well as Langston Hughes, T. S. Eliot as well as John Dos Passos, and branched out into a discussion of that most modern of art forms, the moving pictures. *Atlantvind* was the first of several books by Lundkvist dealing with American literature,[28] and by its assimilation of ideas and manner from that literature for ends of its own, one of the most effective in vitalizing American literature in the consciousness of Swedish authors.

Equally important, though coming a few years later and making its strongest impression upon short story writers, was the Hemingway vogue. Hemingway was first read and imitated in 1933 by Walter Ljungquist. He became in the later 'thirties and early 'forties the center of a cult

[23] Artur Lundkvist, *Atlantvind,* Stockholm, 1932, p. 191.

[24] *Ibid.,* p. 10.

[25] *Ibid.,* p. 18.

[26] *Ibid.,* p. 29.

[27] *Ibid.,* p. 90.

[28] The others are *Tre Amerikaner, op. cit.; Ikarus' flykt,* Stockholm, 1939, containing essays on Eliot, Faulkner, and Henry Miller; *Amerikas nya författare,* Stockholm, 1940 (Studentföreningen Verdandis småskrifter no. 423); and *Diktare och avslöjare i Amerikas moderna litteratur,* Stockholm, 1942. Lundkvist is also the author of scores of reviews and critical essays on American literature appearing in newspapars and literary magazines.

that owed much of its awareness of Hemingway to the critic and short-story writer Thorsten Jonsson and that left its impress upon nearly a dozen Swedish writers.[29] Jonsson's many articles in the Social Democratic magazine *Tiden* and in the Stockholm newspaper *Dagens Nyheter,* of which he became cultural editor in the 'forties, and his books on America and American literature[30] made him a leading spokesman for American culture in the 'forties.

In the midst of such activity—only a few highlights have been suggested here—American Nobel Prize winners came and went: Eugene O'Neill in 1936, Pearl Buck in 1938, T. S. Eliot in 1948, William Faulkner in 1950 (for 1949), and Ernest Hemingway in 1954. Historically, none of these awards has the significance of the award to Lewis in 1930. It was, of course, no less true of the awards to the other Americans than it was of that to Lewis that the Nobel Prize, because it is so highly regarded, enlarges the audience for the kind of work it honors and requires the serious consideration of critics of all colors of belief. Critics and publishers alike subsequently find, therefore, greater freedom in introducing associated writing to that enlarged audience. But even more was implied in the award to Lewis, for it constituted public recognition of the virtual breakdown of the barrier erected before all aspects of American culture by Knut Hamsun and his Swedish successors as much as forty years before. The ceremony over, it was as last possible for criticism and publication to go ahead without apology and without generalized references to the culture of origin. The air was cleared, American literature was on its own and on a par with other literatures. The same effect would doubtless

[29] Artur Lundkvist, "Novellens förnyelse," *ST,* January 14, 1945, is a brief survey of modern Swedish short story writing and its debt to Hemingway and Saroyan. Other contemporary articles suggesting the influence of Hemingway on Swedish novelists as well as short story writers are: Georg Svensson, "Prisromanerna," *Bonniers Litterära Magasin,* II, no. 9 (November 1933), 8—14 (Hemingway's probable influence on Walter Ljungquist's *Ombyte av tåg*); Ivar Harrie, "Svenska romaner och noveller, II," *Ord och Bild,* XLIX (1940), 217—224 (Hemingway's influence on Thorsten Jonsson's *Som det brukar vara*); Örjan Lindberger, "Svenska romaner och noveller 1941," *Ord och Bild,* LI (1942), 418—431 (Hemingway's influence on Thorsten Jonsson's *Fly till vatten och morgon,* Peter Nisser's *Blod och snö,* and Sven Rydberg's *Konversation under en lampa*). G[eorg] S[vensson], "Hemingways mästerverk på svenska," *Bonniers Litterära Magasin,* I, no. 7 (September 1932), 73—74, contains one of the earliest Swedish efforts to define Hemingway's style.

[30] *Sex amerikaner,* Stockholm, 1942 (essays on Hemingway, Faulkner, Steinbeck, Caldwell, Farrell, and Saroyan); *Sidor av Amerika,* Stockholm, 1946 (travel impressions and essays on Scott Fitzgerald, Sandburg, Faulkner, and Cummings); and the posthumous *Synpunkter,* Stockholm, 1951, containing many essays on American literature.

have been achieved by giving the award, say, to Dreiser later or earlier than 1930, but the very nature and history of the Swedish approach to American literature in the 'twenties required that Lewis be the recipient, and it was not until 1930 that that fact became indisputably clear to all, when Lewis had not only *Main Street* and *Babbitt* behind him but *Elmer Gantry* and *Dodsworth* as well. This was the service Lewis performed for American literature in Sweden and indeed wherever the Nobel Prize is held in regard.

Bibliography
and
Appendixes

See Appendix B for bibliography of newspaper reviews and essays for authors and books discussed at length in the text.

Books

AGRELL, SIGURD, *Arabesker*, Stockholm, 1903.

AHLENIUS, HOLGER, *Gustaf Hellström*, Stockholm, 1934 (Studentföreningen Verdandis småskrifter no. 364).

ANDERSSON, NILS, *Dagspressen i Sverige*, Stockholm, 1948.

ANGERED-STRANDBERG, HILMA, *Den nya världen*, Stockholm, 1898.

—— *På prärien*, Stockholm, 1898.

ASPLUND, KARL, and GUNNAR M. SILFVERSTOLPE, *Vers från väster: Modern engelsk och amerikansk lyrik i svensk tolkning*, Stockholm, 1922.

BERG, RUBEN, *Moderna amerikaner*, Stockholm, 1925.

BERGER, HENNING, *Där ute*, ed. Fredrik Böök, Stockholm, 1927.

BERGMAN, HJALMAR, *Dollar: Komedi i tre akter*, Stockholm, 1926.

BÖÖK, FREDRIK, *Essayer och kritiker, 1919—1920*, Stockholm, 1921.

—— *Svenska studier i litteraturvetenskap*, Stockholm, 1913.

BOYE, KARIN, *Härdarna*, Stockholm, 1927.

DIKTONIUS, ELMER, *Ungt hav*, Helsingfors, 1923.

EKELUND, VILHELM, *Böcker och vandringar*, Stockholm, 1923.

ELGSTRÖM, ANNA LENAH, and GUSTAF COLLIJN, *U. S. A.: Liv och teater*, Stockholm, 1927.

ELOVSON, HARALD, *Amerika i svensk litteratur, 1750—1820: En studie i komparativ litteraturhistoria*, Lund, 1930.

HALLSTRÖM, PER, *Vilsna fåglar*, Stockholm, 1894.

—— *Händelser*, Stockholm, 1927.

HAMSUN, KNUT, *Fra det moderne Amerikas Aandsliv*, Copenhagen, 1889.

—— *Hunger*, transl. George Egerton, introd. Edwin Björkman, New York, 1920.

HARRIE, IVAR, *In i fyrtiotalet*, Stockholm, 1944.

—— *Tjugotalet in memoriam*, Stockholm, 1936.

HELLSTRÖM, GUSTAF, *Ett rekommendationsbrev*, Stockholm, 1920.

—— *Förenta staterna och världsfreden*, Stockholm, 1919.

HOLMBERG, OLLE, *Sverige — modell 1933*, Stockholm, 1933.

JAENSSON, KNUT, *Fredrik Böök som litteraturkritiker*, Stockholm, 1939 (Studentföreningen Verdandis småskrifter no. 416).

JONSSON, THORSTEN, *Sex amerikaner: Hemingway, Faulkner, Steinbeck, Caldwell, Farrell, Saroyan,* Stockholm, 1942.

—— *Sidor av Amerika: Intryck och resonemang,* Stockholm, 1946.

—— *Synpunkter,* Stockholm, 1951.

KARLFELDT, ERIK AXEL, *Hösthorn,* Stockholm, 1932.

—— *Why Sinclair Lewis Got the Nobel Prize* ... and Sinclair Lewis, *Address before the Swedish Academy,* New York [n.d.].

KOHT, HALVDAN, *The American Spirit in Europe, A Survey of Transatlantic Influences,* Philadelphia, 1949.

LEMOINE, OSBORNE, *Jack London och hans diktargärning,* Stockholm, 1920.

Les Prix Nobel en 1930, Stockholm, 1931.

LEWIS, SINCLAIR, *The American Fear of Literature,* Stockholm, 1931.

LUNDKVIST, ARTUR, *Amerikas nya författare,* Stockholm, 1940 (Studentföreningen Verdandis småskrifter no. 423).

—— *Atlantvind,* Stockholm, 1932.

—— *Diktare och avslöjare i Amerikas moderna litteratur,* Stockholm, 1942.

—— *Ikarus' flykt,* Stockholm, 1939.

—— *Tre amerikaner: Dreiser, Lewis, Anderson,* Stockholm 1939 (Studentföreningen Verdandis småskrifter, no. 415).

MARBLE, ANNIE RUSSELL, *The Nobel Prize Winners in Literature, 1901—1931,* New York, London, 1932.

NEVINS, ALLAN, comp. and ed., *American Social History as Recorded by British Travellers,* New York, 1923.

OSSIANNILSSON, K. G., *Amerikaner och Byzantiner,* Stockholm, 1905.

SCHÜCK, HENRIK, and KARL WARBURG, *Svensk litteraturhistoria* (3rd ed.), VIII (by Erik Hj. Linder), Stockholm, 1949.

SELANDER, STEN, *Européer, amerikaner, och annat,* Stockholm, 1930.

SKAVLAN, EINAR, *Knut Hamsun,* Oslo, 1929.

The Sweden Year-Book 1938, Uppsala, 1938.

THULSTRUP, ÅKE, *Fredrik Böök som politisk skriftställare,* Stockholm, 1941.

TIGERSTEDT, E. N., *Svensk litteraturhistoria,* Stockholm, 1948.

VAN DOREN, CARL, *Contemporary American Novelists, 1900—1920,* New York, 1923.

Essays, Newspaper Articles, etc.

ASKLUND, ERIK, "Köld och kärlek," *Fönstret,* no. 44—45 (December 17, 1932), p. 11.

"Babbitts far intervjuar mr S. Lewis," *Dagens Nyheter,* December 9, 1920.

"Askungen," "Babbitts författare at home," *Svenska Dagbladet,* June 23, 1929.

BERG, RUBEN, "Förenta staternas moderna dramatik," *Aftonbladet,* April 3, 1922.

—— "En ny amerikansk författarinna," *Aftonbladet,* February 6, 1925.

—— "Den nordamerikanska litteraturen och Sverige," *Nordisk familjeboks månadskrönika,* I (1938), 401—407.

BOLANDER, CARL-AUGUST, "Moderna amerikaner," *Dagens Nyheter*, December 9, 1925.

— "Problemet U. S. A.," *Dagens Nyheter*, December 5, 1927.

BUTENSCHÖN, ANDREA, "Walt Whitman," *Ord och Bild*, XIV (1905), 351—367.

"De populäraste författarna," *Svenska Dagbladet*, December 4, 1915.

"E., P. J.," "Amerikansk Självgodhet, Parlamentariskt Tragglande och Fascistiskt Tyranni Hota den Samtida Kulturvärlden: En intervju med Per Hallström," *Nya Dagligt Allehanda*, January 15, 1928.

ELGSTRÖM, ANNA LENAH, "Babbitt erövraren," *Social-Demokraten*, November 3, 1928.

EMILSON, HÄLGE, "Amerikansk kulturkritik," *Sydsvenska Dagbladet Snällposten*, August 18, 1929.

"Es An," "Moderna amerikaner," *Göteborgs-Posten*, November 17, 1925.

F[OGELQVIS]T, T[ORSTEN], "Sinclair Lewis erhöll årets litteraturpris," *Dagens Nyheter*, November 6, 1930.

"Fyra stormän på andens fält hyllas i vältaliga ordalag i festsal och på bankett," *Dagens Nyheter*, December 11, 1930.

"Grey," "Lewis' Nobeltal är sensation i Amerikapressen," *Svenska Dagbladet*, December 14, 1930.

GRIFFIN, SIR LEPEL, "A Visit to Philistia," *Fortnightly Review*, XLI, n.s. XXXV (January 1884), 50—64.

"Grym salva mot amerikanska realister," *Social-Demokraten*, March 11, 1931.

"H., J. B.," "Den svenska veckopressen och Amerika," *Fönstret*, no. 11 (March 14, 1931), p. 14.

"Hb.," "Nobelt i Allehanda," *Social-Demokraten*, October 11, 1930.

HARRIE, IVAR, "Svenska romaner och noveller, II," *Ord och Bild*, XLIX (1940), 217—224.

HELLSTRÖM, GUSTAF, "'Vilda Västern' i nyare amerikansk litteratur," *Vår Tid*, X (1925), 47—91.

— "Damerna i Porkville," in *Mannen vid ratten,* Stockholm, 1926, pp. 123—135.

H[OLMBER]G, O[LLE], "Fritz Thorén död," *Dagens Nyheter*, February 16, 1950.

JOHANSSON, KLARA, "Amerikanska rebeller," in *Det speglade livet,* Stockholm, 1926, pp. 215—232.

LAURIN, CARL G., "Amerikanismen," *Svenska Dagbladet*, December 19 and 20, 1927.

LEWIS, SINCLAIR, "Självporträtt," transl. Margareta Odelberg, in *P*A*N: vers och prosa*, Stockholm, 1927, pp. 63—77.

— "Mr Babbitt i England," *Svenska Dagbladet*, July 8, 15, 22, 29, August 5, 12, 19, September 2, 9, 16, 23, 1928.

LINDBERGER, ÖRJAN, "Svenska romaner och noveller," *Ord och Bild*, LI (1942), 418—431.

LINDSKOG, O[LE], "Amerikansk civilisation i våra dagar," *Sydsvenska Dagbladet Snällposten*, November 29, 1925.

"Litterära bekymmer i U. S. A. skildras av Sinclair Lewis," *Svenska Dagbladet,* December 13, 1930.

LUNDKVIST, ARTUR, "Nobelpris med adress Amerika," *Fönstret,* no. 29 (November 15, 1930), p. 10.

—— "Novellens förnyelse," *Stockholms-Tidningen,* January 14, 1945.

—— "Amerikas litteratur," in *USA i blickpunkten,* Stockholm, 1949, pp. 321–362.

MÖLLER, ARTUR, "Gustaf Hellström," *Ord och Bild,* XLI (1932), 447–456.

MORTENSEN, JOHAN, "Intryck från nuets U. S. A.," *Sydsvenska Dagbladet Snällposten,* December 21, 1927.

NILSSON-TANNÉR, PER, "Köp svenskt — läs amerikanskt!" *Fönstret,* March 9, 1932.

OLSSON, GUSTAF, "Den tröstlösaste av civilisationer," *Sydsvenska Dagbladet Snällposten,* January 24, 1930.

O[LSSON], H[A]G[A]R, "Walt Whitman föregångaren," *Ultra,* I (October 15, 1922), 44–45.

P[AULI], I[VAN], "Amerikansk självprövning," *Arbetet,* December 12, 1925.

—— "Amerikanska perspektiv," *Social-Demokraten,* December 20, 1927.

"Politiken influerad av mr Lewis," *Dagens Nyheter,* November 26, 1930.

"Pulitzerpriset för 1925 refuserat," *Svenska Dagbladet,* May 10, 1926.

RINMAN, SVEN, "American books translated into Swedish 1945–47," *American-Swedish Handbook,* III (1948), 151–159.

"Sinclair Lewis anlände i natt till Göteborg," *Svenska Dagbladet,* December 9, 1930.

"Sinclair Lewis fick årets litterära nobelpris," *Svenska Dagbladet,* November 6, 1930.

"Sinclair Lewis håller spydigt Nobelföredrag," *Dagens Nyheter,* December 13, 1930.

"Sm," "Författaren för dagen i Amerika," *Svenska Dagbladet,* July 29, 1921.

S[ÖDERHIEL]M, H[ENNING], "Amerikanska författare," *Göteborgs Handels- och Sjöfarts-Tidning,* December 7, 1925.

STARFELT-HALLGREN, VIVEKA, "Amerikansk kulturimport," *Fönstret,* no. 9 (February 28, 1931), p. 4.

"Ståtligt Nobeltåg med bankettdebut i Gyllene salen," *Dagens Nyheter,* December 11, 1930.

S[TRÖMBER]G, KJ[ELL], "Approcessens bakgrund," *Stockholms-Tidningen,* November 22, 1925.

S[VENSSON], G[EORG], "Hemingways mästerverk på svenska," *Bonniers Litterära Magasin,* I, no. 7 (September 1932), 73–74.

—— "Prisromanerna," *Bonniers Litterära Magasin,* II, no. 9 (November 1933), 8–14.

TINGSTEN, HERBERT, "Sinclair Lewis lyckliga år." *Dagens Nyheter,* February 3, 1953.

"U. S. A:s svaghet en modernitet utan innehåll," *Dagens Nyheter,* December 10, 1930.

WAHLSTRÖM, LYDIA, "Det 'gamla' Amerika," *Svenska Morgonbladet*, December 27, 1927.

WERIN, ALGOT, "Per Hallström," *Ord och Bild*, XXXV (1926), 617—628.

WIESELGREN, OSCAR, "Gustaf Hellström," *Biblioteksbladet*, XVI (1932), 5—11.

Note: The following periodicals were examined:

Ateneum, 1933—1935.

Bonniers Litterära Magasin, 1932—1945.

Fönstret, 1930—1933.

Fronten, 1931—1932.

Juvenes dum sumus, 1924—1926.

Karavan, 1934—1935.

Ny generation, 1925.

Ord och Bild, 1905—1942.

Quosego, Tidskrift för en ny generation, 1929.

Spektrum, 1931—1932.

Ultra, Kirjallistaiteell:nen aikakauslehti, Tidskrift för en ny konst och litteratur, 1922.

Books of Fiction by American Authors Translated into Swedish 1916 to 1945, inclusive[1]

Except as noted below, the following list of books of fiction by American authors translated into Swedish is derived exclusively from the *Utländsk skönlitteratur* ("foreign literature in prose") sections of *Svensk bok-katalog*, a cumulative list of publications in Swedish issued every five years, for the years 1916 to 1940, and of *Årskatalog för svenska bokhandeln*, an annual continuation in the same form, for the years 1941 to 1945, inclusive. Unfortunately, translations of fiction appearing in newspapers and magazines could not be included in the list; since these are not indexed in Sweden, the time and effort required to recover them would have been vastly disproportionate to the value of the results to the present study.

In culling the names of American authors from the Swedish catalogs, resort was made for the purpose of identifying lesser known authors to standard biographical dictionaries, to Burke and Howe's *American Authors and Books 1640—1940*, to appropriate volumes of *Who's Who in America* and similar regional publications, and to the *Book Review Digest*. Only those authors were included who could be positively identified as American either by birth or by their being commonly regarded by the available authorities as American by virtue of early naturalization or lengthy sojourn in America during a major part of their writing careers. Three or four doubtful cases that arose in the application of this standard were resolved in favor of making the list as complete as possible, at the risk of course of offending by seeming at times to fling our net too far; although there can be no question that such writers as Herman Landon and Gösta Larsson, having come to America in their early years, are properly included, the case admittedly grows weaker for the inclusion of such a writer as Hugh Lofting in spite of his very lengthy tour in America, and seemed in-

---

[1] Sven Rinman, "American books translated into Swedish 1945–47," *American-Swedish Handbook,* III (1948), 151—159 (Rock Island, Illinois), may be consulted as a continuation of the present survey.

defensible for such a writer as Vicki Baum, who in spite of American naturalization is excluded from the list on the basis of language, subject matter, writing career abroad, and reputation. There was inevitably also a handful of writers who gave some indication from their publication records of being American but who have apparently left no biographical trace behind them, and these writers, like Mildred Barbour, author of *Sibyl, Trapper of Men,* and Adele Knight, author of *Mademoiselle Celeste,* are not included, probably without serious loss. Since the reception of Jack London's and Upton Sinclair's books is discussed in some detail in the text, an exception to the general procedure has been made in listing *all* translations of their books, fiction and non-fiction alike, including those published earlier than 1916.

The manner of listing is alphabetical by author for the entire period covered; the translations of each author are arranged chronologically by year of publication in Swedish. Authors' names are given as usually listed in standard reference works, and pseudonyms, if any, follow in quotation marks within parentheses. The Swedish title, publisher, and year of publication then follow; unless otherwise specified, the place of publication is always Stockholm, More than one edition or printing (the Swedish catalogs do not differentiate between the two) of a book in a single year is indicated in parentheses after the year in question, and editions or reprints in subsequent years are shown merely by listing the year or years such editions or reprints appeared. Whenever possible, only one entry for each book is made even though the Swedish title may have been changed in later editions; however, Jack London's books were issued under such a variety of titles by a large number of publishers that it has not been possible to ascertain, without consulting each of the volumes in question, if some of the volumes separately listed do not actually constitute later editions; the same difficulties apply to the collections of Poe's short stories, which were sometimes given identical titles by different publishers although the contents varied from book to book. In both cases, when there has been no positive means of identifying the originals of the volumes in question, the titles have been separately listed.

As the list shows, the amount of translation was not inconsiderable at any time, yet only in the late 'thirties and in the 'forties did it increase sufficiently to compare with the rate of translation into Swedish of other foreign literature, particularly those of the other Scandinavian countries,

France, and Germany. If one were to remove from one's calculations the very numerous translations of Jack London as being an anomalous phenomenon not of a piece with the general trend, a curve might be drawn based on quantity of translation that would rise sharply from 1916 to 1920, continue erratically and slowly to rise still higher in the 1920's, recede in the early 'thirties, and then surge upward to its greatest height in 1944, when editions of American books in translation numbered 81.

Qualitatively, although many important writers were translated, Westerns, adventure stories, travel stories, and the like preponderated in the early years, and most often even the best that was then translated did not appear in Swedish until many years—as much as thirty and forty in some instances—after publication in the original. Sinclair Lewis was a very notable exception; Edith Wharton, for example, whose *House of Mirth* was seventeen years old when translated in 1922, was not. Toward the end of the 'twenties, however, it obviously had become increasingly incumbent upon publishers to keep abreast with activities across the Atlantic, and from that time on the lag in Swedish translation behind American publication diminished to a point where American books today are translated within a few months of their American appearance. The creation of a new audience in Sweden for American fiction during this period, an achievement to be credited mainly to the reception of Sinclair Lewis's novels, also resulted in the gradual diminution of the relative importance, quantitatively, of the Rex Beaches, James Curwoods, Archibald Gunters, and Jean Websters; by the 'thirties the bulk of translation was made up of books by such writers as Louis Bromfield, Edna Ferber, Pearl Buck, Nordhoff and Hall, Peter B. Kyne, and of course Sinclair Lewis. At the same time publishers assumed a responsibility that they had seldom exercised, or had cause to exercise before in bringing as quickly as possible to their readers even the less popular writers of merit; Faulkner, Dos Passos, and even Dreiser undoubtedly were translated with expectation of considerable financial risk, although the latter, possibly through his becoming involved in the Nobel Prize discussions of 1930, paid his way, if no more. By the 'forties publishers were willing to take on such a formidable task as translating for the first time *Moby-Dick* and to make a novel by Henry James once more available.

The list that follows clearly shows, in other words, that not merely among critics, students, and other special readers, but also among publishers, faced with harsher considerations in choosing additions for their lists, and hence among their clients, there was in the period after World

War I a growing awareness of the existence of an important body of literature in the United States. Although more than half of the American authors on the list are represented by only one or two translations, probably quickly read and quickly forgotten, the whole body of translations, capped as it had now been by selections from the best of American literature past and present, was finally enough to sustain the hard-won general conviction that American literature has an undisputed place in world literature and a promise to fulfill.

ABBOTT, ELEANOR, *Molly Munter*, Fahlcrantz, 1921.

ADAMS, SAMUEL H., *Spelet kring Vita huset*, Norstedt, 1927.

ALBRAND, MARTHA, *Det hände i Holland*, Tiden, 1943.

ALDRICH, BESS S., *Den brinnande lågan*, Saxon & Lindström, 1944.

ALEXANDER, CHARLES, *Bobbie, en fårhunds historia*, Hökerberg, 1927.

ALGREN, NELSON, *Det gryr ingen morgon*, Wahlström & Widstrand, 1945.

ALLEE, MARJORIE, *En länk i kedjan*, Natur och Kultur, 1942.

ALLEN, JAMES L., *Den osynliga kören*, Åhlén & Åkerlund, 1925.

ALLEN, HERVEY, *Anthony Adverse*, Norstedt, vol. I, 1934 (3 eds.), 1937; vol. II, 1934 (2 eds.), 1936; vol. III, 1934 (2 eds.), 1937.

—— *Det hände vid Aquila*, Norstedt, 1938 (2 eds.).

—— *Fortet i skogen*, Norstedt, 1944.

—— *Värdshuset i vildmarken*, Norstedt, 1945.

ANDERSON, SHERWOOD, *Mannen från västern*, Tiden, 1928.

—— *Mörkt skratt*, Bonnier, 1928.

ASCH, NATHAN, *Kontoret*, Bonnier, 1927.

ATHERTON, GERTRUDE, *Fången eller fri*, B. Wahlström, 1916.

—— *Hans härskarinna*, Göteborg: Västra Sverige, 1916.

—— *Den förtrollade ön*, Dahlberg, 1919.

—— *Ett giftermål av höjelse*, B. Wahlström, 1919.

—— *Vad kvinnan vill ...*, B. Wahlström, 1920.

AUSTIN, ANNIE, *Passion*, Bästa böcker, 1933.

—— *Naomi*, Åhlén & söner, 1936.

BAILEY, TEMPLE, *Blå fönstret*, Hökerberg, 1927.

—— *Flickorna Claybourne*, Hökerberg, 1928.

—— *Valet*, Hökerberg, 1929.

BALDWIN, FAITH, *Nygifta*, Hökerberg, 1932 (3 eds.).

—— *Skönhet*, Bonnier, 1934, 1937, 1939.

BALDWIN, FAITH, *Kontorshustrun*, Bonnier, 1935; Åhlén & Åkerlund, 1939.

—— *Jag vill ha kvar min plats!* Bonnier, 1937.

Den andra mannen, Bonnier, 1939.

BANGS, JOHN K., *En lustbåt på Styx*, Wahlström & Widstrand, 1917.

BARBOUR, RALPH H., *Lilla nåden*, Nordiska förlaget, 1919.

BARNES, MARGARET A., *Från vår till höst*, Bonnier, 1934.

—— *Ombord på Atlanta*, Skoglund, 1939.

—— *Visdomens port*, Skoglund, 1939.

BARRETT, WILLIAM K., *Kvinnan bakom diktatorn*, Fahlcrantz & Gumælius, 1939.

BARTLETT, FREDERICK, *Leken blev allvar*, Fritze, 1920.

—— *Flickan från Wall Street*, Åhlén & Åkerlund, 1922.

—— *Joan & Co.*, Fritze, 1925.

BAUR, BETTY, *Den vita drottningen*, Norstedt, 1944.

BEACH, REX, *Äventyrare*, Bonnier, 1917, 1918 (2 eds.); Holmquist, 1922, 1925.

—— *Skiljemuren*, Bonnier, 1918; Vårt hem, 1928.

—— *Silverstimmet i Alaska*, Åhlén & Åkerlund, 1919; B. Wahlström, 1936, 1940.

—— *Den ensamma stjärnan*, Åhlén & Åkerlund, 1920 (2 eds.).

—— *Kastvindar*, Bonnier, 1920.

—— *Skrattande Bill*, Bonnier, 1921.

—— *Halvblodsindianskan*, Holmquist, 1922, 1925.

—— *Nätet*, Åhlén & Åkerlund, 1922.

—— *Kompanjoner*, Holmquist, 1923.

—— *Människan spår*, Åhlén & Åkerlund, 1923.

—— *Guldgrävarlägrets dotter*, Nutiden, 1927.

—— *Guldgrävarens kärlekssaga*, Saxon & Lindström, 1936.

—— *Alaskaflickan*, B. Wahlström, 1938, 1940.

—— *Vid nordlandets gräns*, B. Wahlström, 1940.

BEECKMAN, ROSS, *Prinsessan Zara*, Nordiska förlaget, 1917.

BELLAMANN, HENRY, *Ringar på vattnet*, Medén, 1940.

—— *En man och hans hus*, Medén, 1944.

BELLAMY, EDWARD, *Vattentornet*, Karlstad: Klasskampens förlag, 1918.

—— *En återblick*, Björck & Börjesson, 1919.

BEMELMANS, LUDWIG, *Hotel Splendide*, Geber, 1943.

BERCOVICI, KONRAD, *Ropet från Volga*, Bonnier, 1926.

BIGELOW, EDITH E., *En medelväg*, Vårt hem, 1926.

BIGGERS, EARL D., *De sju breven*, Dahlberg, 1918.

—— *Den kinesiska papegojan*, Almqvist & Wiksell, 1927; B. Wahlström, 1937.

—— *Sammetstofflorna*, Schildt, 1929.

—— *Den svarta kamelen*, Schildt, 1931; B. Wahlström, 1936.

—— *Charlie Chan griper in*, Bonnier, 1934, 1940, 1941; Åhlén & Åkerlund, vols. I and II, 1937; vol. II, 1938.

—— Charlie Chan på semester, *Bonnier*, 1936.

—— *Charlie Chans triumf*, B. Wahlström, 1938, 1941.

BINNS, ARCHIE, *Obruten mark*, Sohlman, 1943.

BLAKE, GLADYS, *Den hemlighetsfulla inskriptionen*, Nordisk rotogravyr, 1928.

BOOTH, CHARLES G., *Generalen dog i gryningen*, Norstedt, 1937.

BRADY, CYRUS T., *För hennes skull,* Holmquist, 1917.
— *I hemliga polisens tjänst,* Nordiska förlaget, 1917.
— *En mot alla,* Nordiska förlaget, 1918.
— *För sonens ära,* B. Wahlström, 1920.
BRAINERD, ELEANOR H., *Hur kunde hon?* Norstedt, 1922.
BRAND, MILLEN, *Åter till livet,* Bonnier, 1938.
BRETHERTON, VIVIEN R., *Berget och vinden,* Natur och Kultur, 1944.
BRIGGS, OLIVE M., *Hemliga makter,* Nordiska förlaget, 1918.
BRINIG, MYRON, *Två kvinnor,* Hökerberg, 1942.
— *Anne Minton,* Hökerberg, 1944.
BRISTOW, GWEN, *Högsommar,* Norstedt, 1938, 1939, 1944.
— *Stora vägen,* Norstedt, 1939 (2 eds.).
— *Farväl till den gamla goda tiden,* Norstedt, 1940 (2 eds.).
— *I morgon och för alltid,* Norstedt, 1944.
BROMFIELD, LOUIS, *Den sällsamma historien om miss Annie Spragg,* Bonnier, 1929,
  1937, 1938, 1939.
— *Tjugofyra timmar,* Bonnier, 1931, 1932, 1933, 1936, 1937, 1938, 1939, 1941.
— *Tidig höst,* Bonnier, 1932 (3 eds.).
— *En modern hjälte,* Bonnier, 1933, 1934.
— *I dag röd — i morgon död,* Bonnier, 1934.
— *Så måste det gå,* Bonnier, 1937 (2 eds.).
— *När regnet kom,* Bonnier, 1938, 1939, 1940, 1944.
— *Beppos nattklubb,* Bonnier, 1940.
— *Natt i Bombay,* Bonnier, 1941 (2 eds.); Åhlén & Åkerlund, 1942.
— *Floden stiger,* Bonnier, 1942.
— *Tills dagen gryr,* Bonnier, 1943.
— *Mrs Parkington,* Bonnier, 1944.
— *Vad blev det av Anna Bolton,* Bonnier, 1945.
BROOKS, ANNE, *Det som håller,* Hökerberg, 1942.
BROWN, ZENITH J. ("David Frome"), *Mr Simpsons fynd,* Tiden, 1933.
— *De blå skorna,* Tiden, 1937.
BROWNE, BELMORE, *Jakten efter guld,* Wahlström & Widstrand, 1919.
BROWNE, LEWIS, *Ivan i Guds eget land,* Hökerberg, 1939.
BUCK, PEARL S., *Den goda jorden,* Hökerberg, 1932 (7 eds.), 1933 (3 eds.), 1938, 1939.
— *Den unge revolutionären,* Bonnier, 1933, 1934, 1937, 1939
— *Östanvind–västanvind,* Bonnier, 1933 (2 eds.).
— *Sönerna,* Hökerberg, 1933, 1938.
— *Modern,* Hökerberg, 1934 (7 eds.); Saxon & Lindström, 1939.
— *Wang Lungs barnbarn,* Hökerberg, 1935 (7 eds.).
— *I fjärran land,* Bonnier, 1937 (3 eds.), 1938.
— *Kämpande ängel,* Bonnier, 1937 (2 eds.), 1938, 1939.
— *Den första hustrun,* Hökerberg, 1938, 1939.

—— *Du stolta hjärta,* Bonnier, 1938, 1939.

—— *Patrioten,* Bonnier, 1939 (2 eds.), 1942.

—— *Andra gudar,* Bonnier, 1940 (2 eds.).

—— *Draksådd,* Bonnier, 1942 (2 eds.).

—— *Löftet,* Bonnier, 1944 (2 eds.).

BULLITT, WILLIAM C., *Huset vid torget,* J. Beckman, 1928.

BURNETT, FRANCES H., *Lille lorden,* Bonnier, 1916.

—— *Hjärtan som mötas,* Holmquist, 1916.

—— *Oväntad lycka,* B. Wahlström, 1916.

—— *Pepita,* B. Wahlström, 1916.

—— *Vad kärleken förmår,* B. Wahlström, 1916.

—— *Dyrköpt lycka,* B. Wahlström, 1917.

—— *Ett brustet hjärta,* B. Wahlström, 1917.

—— *Skottspolen,* Bonnier, 1917.

—— *En lyckad guldgosse,* Bonnier, 1918.

—— *Häxan,* B. Wahlström, 1920.

—— *Ätten Coombes huvudman,* Bonnier, 1923.

—— *Robin,* Bonnier, 1923.

—— *Markisinnan,* Bonnier, 1924.

—— *Mannen utan morgondag,* Fahlcrantz, 1927.

BURNETT, W. R., *Chicago-Caesar,* Sigillet, 1941.

BURRAGE, HENRY S., *Trogen intill döden,* B. M:s bokförlag, 1923.

BURROUGHS, EDGAR R., *Den vansinnige kungen,* Göteborg: Västra Sverige, 1920.

—— *Tarzan, apornas son,* Hökerberg, 1921, 1922, 1923, 1936.

—— *Tarzans återkomst,* Hökerberg, 1921, 1924, 1927.

—— *Starka Billy,* Hökerberg, 1922.

—— *Tarzans son,* Hökerberg, 1922, 1924, 1926.

—— *Tarzans vilda vänner,* Hökerberg, 1922, 1923.

—— *Starka Billy på äventyr,* Hökerberg, 1923.

—— *Tarzan och den vita kvinnan,* Hökerberg, 1923, 1926.

—— *Tarzan och Opars diamanter,* Hökerberg, 1923.

—— *Prinsessan av Mars,* Hökerberg, 1924.

—— *Prinsessan av Mars befrias,* Hökerberg, 1924.

—— *Tarzans hjärta talar,* Hökerberg, 1924.

—— *Tarzan och urfolket,* Hökerberg, 1924, 1927.

—— *Filmflickan från Hollywood,* Hökerberg, 1926.

—— *Tarzan och dvärgfolket,* Hökerberg, 1926, 1927.

—— *Tarzan och det gyllene lejonet,* Hökerberg, 1927.

BURTIS, THOMSON, *Russ Farrell, Flygaren,* Chelius, 1930 (2 eds.).

—— *Russ Farrell, Gränspatrullen,* Chelius, 1930.

—— *Russ Farrell, Konstflygaren,* Chelius, 1930.

—— *Russ Farrell, Tävlingsflygaren,* Chelius, 1930.

BYRNE, DONN, *Det stora grå huset*, Geber, 1928.
CAIN, JAMES M., *Blindstyre*, Universal Press, 1935.
—— *Serenad*, Wahlström & Widstrand, 1938.
—— *En amerikansk kvinna*, Tiden, 1942, 1944.
CALDWELL, ERSKINE, *Snälla vita herrar*, Uppsala: Nyblom, 1942.
—— *Son av Georgia*, Forum, 1945.
—— *Tobaksvägen*, Fritze, 1945.
CALDWELL, TAYLOR, *Dödens dynasti*, Medén, 1939.
—— *Jag och Lasarus*, Medén, 1941.
—— *Jorden är Herrens*, Medén, 1942.
—— *Porträtt i grönt*, Medén, 1943.
—— *Att icke hava kärlek*, Wahlström & Widstrand, 1945.
CARLISLE, HELEN G., *Livet bär mig*, Wahlström & Widstrand, 1934.
CARPENTER, MARGARET, *Väldigt experiment*, Ljus, 1944 (2 eds.).
CARR, JOHN D., *Tusen-och-en-natt-mysteriet*, Skoglund, 1936.
—— *Svart sabbat*, Bonnier, 1939.
—— *Det krökta gångjärnet*, Bonnier, 1940.
—— *Väck ej de döda!* Bonnier, 1940.
—— *Mördaren skipar rättvisa*, Bonnier, 1945.
CARR, ROBERT S., *16, 17, 18 år*, Bonnier, 1929.
CARROLL, GLADYS H., *Sol över fälten*, Bonnier, 1935.
CASPARY, VERA, *Laura*, Forum, 1945.
CATHER, WILLA S., *Hell, banbrytare!* Fritze, 1919.
—— *Banbrytare*, Saxon & Lindström, 1943.
—— *Lärksången*, Fritze, 1920.
—— *Ett förlorat ideal*, Norstedt, 1924.
—— *Professorns hem*, Geber, 1927.
—— *Av allt ditt hjärta*, Geber, 1936.
—— *Landet långt borta*, Geber, 1938 (2 eds.).
—— *Min Antonia*, Geber, 1939 (2 eds.).
—— *Skuggor över klippan*, Geber, 1940.
—— *Sapphira och slavinnan*, Geber, 1941.
CHAMBERLAIN, WILLIAM W., *Gyllene skördar*, Fahlcrantz & Gumælius, 1944.
CHAMBERS, ROBERT W., *Den farliga gränsen*, Bonnier, 1919.
—— *Det oroliga könet*, Bonnier, 1920.
—— *Modellen från gatan*, Nutiden, 1927.
CHASE, MARY E., *Stormhällan*, Uppsala: Lindblad, 1943.
CHEVALIER, ELIZABETH P., *Okuvlig kvinna*, Forum, 1945.
CLARK, WALTER V. T., *Möte vid Oxoket*, Bonnier, 1944.
CLEMENS, SAMUEL L. ("Mark Twain"), *Huckleberry Finns äventyr*, Björck & Börjesson, 1919, 1940; B. Wahlström, 1928.
—— *Tom Sawyers äventyr*, Björck & Börjesson, 1919; Åhlén & Åkerlund, 1920; B. Wahlström, 1928.

—— *Tom Sawyer som detektiv, Tom Sawyer på resa,* Björck & Börjesson, 1919.

—— *Tom Sawyer som detektiv, Också en detektivhistoria,* B. Wahlström, 1929.

—— *Lustiga historier,* Björck & Börjesson, 1922.

—— *En yankee vid kung Arturs hov,* Björck & Börjesson, 1916.

—— *En droppe negerblod,* Björck & Börjesson, 1918, 1919; B. Wahlström, 1929.

—— *Spionen från Louisiana och andra humoresker,* Nutiden, 1918.

—— *Guldgrävarkatten,* Dahlberg, 1919.

—— *På Mississippifloden,* Björck & Börjesson, 1919.

—— *Prinsen och tiggargossen,* Björck & Börjesson, 1919; *Prinsen och tiggaren,* B. Wahlström, 1928.

—— *En amerikansk valkampanj och andra humoresker,* Rabén & Sjögren, 1944.

—— *Jeanne d'Arc,* Lindfors, 1945.

COBB, HUMPHREY, *På ärans fält,* Geber, 1935.

COLEBROOK, JOAN, *En gång trodde vi . . .,* Geber, 1942.

COMFORT, WILL L., *Krigskorrespondentens förräderi,* Nordiska förlaget, 1917.

CONNELL, RICHARD E., *Detektiv till sjöss,* Schildt, 1934; J. Hasselgren, 1942.

COOKE, MARJORIE B., *Bambi,* Svenska andelsförlaget, 1917, 1918, 1921, 1927.

—— *Jane askungen,* Svenska andelsförlaget, 1920 (2 eds.), 1927.

—— *Syrsan,* Svenska andelsförlaget, 1920, 1921.

—— *Flickan som bodde i skogen,* Svenska andelsförlaget, 1921.

COOPER, J. FENIMORE, *Den siste mohikanen,* Björck & Börjesson, 1916, 1928; Biblioteksförlaget, 1926.

—— *Vägvisaren,* Björck & Börjesson, 1916.

—— *Skinnstrumpa,* Björck & Börjesson, 1917.

—— *Prärien,* Björck & Börjesson, 1918.

—— *Hjortdödaren,* Björck & Börjesson, 1919.

—— *Nybyggarna vid Wish-Ton-Wish,* Holmquist, 1919.

—— *Spejaren,* Holmquist, 1919.

CORCORAN, WILLIAM, *En man och hans kärlek,* Hökerberg, 1938 (2 eds.).

COSTAIN, THOMAS B., *Hav, öppna dig!* Wahlström & Widstrand, 1944.

COURNOS, JOHN, *Sådant är livet,* Hökerberg, 1928.

COZZENS, JAMES G., *S. S. San Pedro,* Bonnier, 1934.

—— *När lagen griper in,* Ljus, 1943.

CRAWFORD, F. MARION, *En ros från i går,* B. Wahlström, 1916.

—— *I brottets skugga,* Nordiska förlaget, 1918.

—— *Den förälskade Mr Isaacs,* B. Wahlström, 1920.

—— *Sant' Ilario,* Oskar Eklund, 1923.

CUMMINS, MARIA S., *Lykttändaren,* Diakonistyrelsen, 1926.

CURWOOD, JAMES O., *Jack Howlands äventyr,* B. Wahlström, 1924, 1928.

—— *Vildmarkens dotter,* B. Wahlström, 1924, 1928, 1933; Bonnier, 1930.

—— *Kazan,* B. Wahlström, 1927, 1928.

—— *Griselbjörnen,* Dahlberg, 1920; B. Wahlström, 1929.

Dos Passos, John, *Till Manhattan*, Bonnier, 1931.
— *42:a breddgraden*, Bonnier, 1932 (2 eds.).
— *1919*, Bonnier, 1939.
Douglas, Lloyd C., *Och förlåt oss våra skulder*, Bonnier, 1934.
— *Nu börjar livet*, Hökerberg, 1941.
— *Icke av denna världen*, Hökerberg, 1944.
Dreiser, Theodore, *En amerikansk tragedi*, Norstedt, 1927.
— *Syster Carrie*, Norstedt, 1928.
— *Finansmannen*, Norstedt, 1929.
— *Jennie Gerhardt*, Norstedt, 1930.
— *Titanen*, Norstedt, 1930.
— *Geniet*, Norstedt, 1936.
Du Bois, Theodora, *Brott i sol*, Geber, 1943.
— *Brott i vitt*, Geber, 1943.
— *Brott i frack*, Geber, 1944.
Duffus, Robert L., *I morgon kommer aldrig*, Bonnier, 1932, 1940.
— *Karavanen går mot väster*, Bonnier, 1936.
Dunn, Joseph A., *Lao-Tzes blomblad*, B. Wahlström, 1920.
Eberhart, Mignon G., *Medan patienten sov*, Wahlström & Widstrand, 1931.
— *Vem sköt?* Wahlström & Widstrand, 1932.
— *Den mörka trappan*, Wahlström & Widstrand, 1933.
— *Veronal*, Wahlström & Widstrand, 1934.
Edmonds, Walter D., *Den glömda dalen*, Uppsala: Lindblad, 1938.
— *Cirkus kommer till sta'n*, Geber, 1942.
— *Firmans yngste*, Uppsala: Lindblad, 1944.
Ehrlich, Leonard, *Guds vredes man*, Skoglund, 1934.
Ellis, J. Breckenridge, *Gladiatorns son: Abnak Ben Samuel*, Nordisk rotogravyr, 1932.
Ellsberg, Edward, *Kapten Paul*, Bonnier, 1943.
English, Judith Kelly, *Äktenskapet — en privat sak?* Ljus, 1944.
Erskine, John, *Den sköna Helenas privatliv*, Hökerberg, 1926.
— *De gyllene portarna*, Schildt, 1934.
— *Margaret Doratts hemlighet*, Hökerberg, 1942.
Estes, Harlow, *Det hände en week-end*, Skoglund, 1943.
— *Hildreth*, Skoglund, 1944.
Farrell, James T., *Studs Lonigan och hans gäng*, Hökerberg, 1939.
Fast, Howard, *I frihetens namn*, Geber, 1941.
— *Tom Paine*, Geber, 1945.
Faulkner, John, *Lättjans vin*, Sohlman, 1944.
Faulkner, William, *Ljus i augusti*, Bonnier, 1944.
Faust, Frederick ("Max Brand"), *Tigern*, Göteborg: Ewald Elander, 1930.
Fenollosa, Mary M. ("Sidney McCall"), *Marias hemlighet*, Nordiska förlaget, 1918.

FERBER, EDNA, *Hennes sons framgång,* Geber, 1925.
—— *Flickorna,* Geber, 1926.
—— *Teaterbåten,* Geber, 1927.
—— *Cimarron,* Bonnier, 1931, 1937; Åhlén & Åkerlund, 1939.
—— *Kom och ta för er!* Bonnier, 1936.
—— *Högt spel i Saratoga,* Bonnier, 1944.
—— *Av fädernas ätt,* Bonnier, 1945.
FERGUSSON, HARVEY, *Segrarnas ättling,* Norstedt, 1923.
FIELD, RACHEL, *Allt detta och himlen därtill,* Bonnier, 1939, 1940, 1942.
—— *Redo för morgondagen,* Bonnier, 1943.
FINEMAN, IRVING, *Doktor Addams,* Geber, 1941.
FISHER, DOROTHY CANFIELD, *Livslycka,* Skoglund, 1922.
FITZGERALD, F. SCOTT, *En man utan skrupler,* Wahlström & Widstrand, 1928.
FLAVIN, MARTIN, *Mr Littlejohn och livet,* Ljus, 1941.
—— *Resa i mörker,* Ljus, 1945.
FLETCHER, INGLIS, *Så föddes en nation,* Ljus, 1941.
—— *Förtrollad jord,* Ljus, 1942.
—— *Frihetens kavaljerer,* Ljus, 1943.
—— *Förlig vind till Caroline,* Ljus, 1945.
FORBES, ESTHER, *En spegel för häxor,* Natur och Kultur, 1929.
FORMAN, JUSTUS M., *Kärlekens stadier,* Fahlcrantz, 1917.
FORRESTER, IZOLA L., *En nyck av ödet,* B. Wahlström, 1916.
FOSTER, MICHAEL, *Amerikansk dröm,* Skoglund, 1939.
FRANKEN, ROSE D., *Claudia,* Bennett, 1940; Nyman, 1942.
—— *Claudia skrattar och gråter,* Wahlström & Widstrand, 1944.
FUCHS, DANIEL, *Förlåt oss våra synder,* Norstedt, 1938.
FUTRELLE, MAY, *Privatsekreteraren,* Nordiska förlaget, 1918.
FUTRELLE, JACQUES, *Mästerdetektiven,* B. Wahlström, 1922, 1929.
—— *Vem vinner?* B. Wahlström, 1922.
GAITHER, FRANCES O., *Den röde hanen gal,* Forum, 1945.
—— *De röda pilarna,* Hasselgren, 1945.
GALLICO, PAUL, *Hemlig front,* Tiden, 1944.
—— *Vingar över Dunkerque,* Världspressen, 1944.
GARDNER, ERLE S., *Fallet Cartright,* Åhlén & söner, 1936; Norrköping: Sörlin, 1941.
—— *Fallet Crocker,* Åhlén & söner, 1936; Norrköping: Sörlin, 1941.
—— *Fallet Brunold,* Åhlén & söner, 1937; Norrköping: Sörlin, 1941.
—— *Fallet Laxter,* Åhlén & söner, 1937; Norrköping: Sörlin, 1941.
—— *Fallet Kent,* Norrköping: Sörlin, 1941.
—— *Mysteriet med kleptomanens sko,* Bonnier, 1941.
—— *Tidvattensmysteriet,* Bonnier, 1943.
GARTH, DAVID, *Fyra om hämnden,* B. Wahlström, 1944.
GELLHORN, MARTHA, *Liana,* Norstedt, 1944.

GIBBS, GEORGE F., *Vägen till Bagdad,* B. Wahlström, 1943.

GILL, THOMAS H., *En skogens son,* Göteborg: Tidsfördrif, 1939.

GLASGOW, ELLEN, *Mannens andra ungdom,* Hökerberg, 1928.

—— *Familjen Littlepage och lyckan,* Hökerberg, 1930.

—— *I lugnt vatten,* Norstedt, 1933.

—— *I detta vårt liv,* Bonnier, 1942.

GOLD, MICHAEL, *Judar utan pengar,* Bonnier, 1931, 1937, 1939.

GOODRICH, MARCUS A., *Delilah,* Norstedt, 1941.

GOODWIN, MAUD WILDER, *Stephen Loring,* Nordiska förlaget, 1919.

GRAY, JAMES, *Livet är värt att leva,* Hökerberg, 1941.

GREGORY, JACKSON, *Vargar,* Bonnier, 1920.

GREY, ZANE, *Ökenfolket,* Bonnier, 1923.

—— *Skogarnas son,* Vårt hem, 1923, 1924.

—— *Purpurviddernas ryttare,* Bonnier, 1924.

—— *Dödsvinden,* Holmquist, 1925.

—— *Regnbågsstigen,* Bonnier, 1925.

—— *Det sista spåret,* Nutiden, 1927.

GROPPER, MILTON H., *Bara en slinka,* Bästa böcker, 1932.

GROSECLOSE, ELGIN, *Ararat,* Fahlcrantz & Gumælius, 1940.

GUNTER, ARCHIBALD C., *Baronessan de Portalis från Sevres,* Holmquist, 1920, 1923.

—— *Billy Hamiltons vackra fånge,* Holmquist, 1920, 1923.

—— *Doktor Burton från New York,* Holmquist, 1920, 1924.

—— *Don Balasco från Key West,* Holmquist, 1920, 1924; Halmstad: Hallandsposten, 1928.

—— *Fasans nätter,* Holmquist, 1920, 1923.

—— *Hennes senator,* Holmquist, 1920, 1925.

—— *I spanjorernas våld,* Holmquist, 1920, 1923.

—— *Kaparkaptenens äventyr,* Holmquist, 1920, 1924.

—— *Kopparprinsessan,* Holmquist, 1920, 1922.

—— *Mademoiselle de Brécourt,* Holmquist, 1920, 1923.

—— *Miss Hammond,* Holmquist, 1920, 1924.

—— *Miss Ingen Alls från Ingen Stans,* Holmquist, 1920, 1922.

—— *Mormonprästens dotter,* Holmquist, 1920, 1923.

—— *Mr Covington från Kentucky,* Holmquist, 1920, 1924.

—— *Mrs Fairbanks,* Holmquist, 1920, 1922.

—— *Ballyho Boy,* Holmquist, 1921, 1923.

—— *Chevalier Gaston från Vesuvius,* Holmquist, 1921.

—— *Hur jag lyckades fly,* Holmquist, 1921, 1924.

—— *Kapten Katsuma från Japan,* Holmquist, 1921.

—— *Kungens bankir,* Holmquist, 1921, 1924.

—— *Miss Forrest,* Holmquist, 1921.

—— *Miss Godfrey från Texas,* Holmquist, 1921.

—— *Miss Pierson från Connecticut,* Holmquist, 1921.
—— *Miss Turnbull från London,* Holmquist, 1921, 1923.
—— *Mr Conway från Nordamerika,* Holmquist, 1921.
—— *Mr Curzon från Hongkong,* Holmquist, 1921.
—— *Mr Lawrence Talbot från Florida,* Holmquist, 1921.
—— *Mr Potter från Texas,* Holmquist, 1921, 1925.
—— *Prins Sendai,* Holmquist, 1921, 1924.
—— *Prinsessan av Paris,* Holmquist, 1921, 1923.
—— *Al-Mansurs kärleksäventyr,* Holmquist, 1922.
—— *Miss Bulgers från Newyork,* Holmquist, 1922, 1924.
—— *M. S. Bradford i Newyork,* Holmquist, 1923.
—— *Mellan svärd och handske,* Holmquist, 1924.
HALL, JAMES N., *Doktor Dogbodys ben,* Bonnier, 1941.
HALL, JOSEF W. ("Upton Close"), *Månflickan,* Geber, 1929.
HALPER, ALBERT, *Klichéfabriken,* Bonnier, 1937.
HAMMETT, DASHIELL, *Den gäckande skuggan,* Skoglund, 1934.
—— *Malteserfalken,* Skoglund, 1935.
HANNA, EVELYN I., *Av samma väv som drömmar,* Medén, 1941.
HARRIS, ANNE COLVER, *Lincolns hustru,* Natur och Kultur, 1944.
HART, FRANCES N., *Bellamyprocessen,* Bonnier, 1930.
HARTE, BRET, *Franciska,* Holmquist, 1916.
—— *Revolutionsgeneralen,* Nutiden, 1918.
—— *Clarence Brants fiende,* Lindström, 1924.
—— *Sovande vattnet,* Nutiden, 1924.
—— *Guldgrävarhistorier,* Åhlén & söner, 1937.
HASKELL, HELEN E., *Katrinka,* Natur och Kultur, 1939.
HAWTHORNE, JULIAN, *Cigarrettfodralet,* B. Wahlström, 1917.
—— *Den stora bankstölden,* B. Wahlström, 1923.
HAWTHORNE, NATHANIEL, *Den eldröda bokstaven,* Uppsala: Lindblad, 1916; Natur
  och Kultur, 1945.
HEMINGWAY, ERNEST, *Och solen går sin gång,* Schildt, 1929.
—— *Farväl till vapnen,* Bonnier, 1932, 1943; Åhlén & Åkerlund, 1941.
—— *Att ha och inte ha,* Bonnier, 1939.
—— *Klockan klämtar för dig,* Bonnier, 1941, 1942; Forum, 1944.
—— *Snön på Kilimandjaro och andra noveller,* Bonnier, 1949
HERGESHEIMER, JOSEPH, *Ammidons hus,* Bonnier, 1920.
—— *Släkten Penny,* Bonnier, 1921.
—— *Dockan,* Bonnier, 1923.
—— *Ludowika Winscombe,* Bonnier, 1924.
—— *Den brokiga schalen,* Bonnier, 1926.
HERMAN, FREDERICK S., *Dynamit i lasten,* Bonnier, 1943.
HERRICK, ROBERT, *En amerikan,* Bonnier, 1917.

HERRMANN, JOHN, *En handelsresande gifter sig,* Fahlcrantz & Gumælius, 1939.

HERSEY, JOHN, *Klockan i Adano,* Norstedt, 1944.

HEYWARD, DU BOSE, *Porgy,* Bonnier, 1930, 1931.

HIGHET, HELEN McINNES, *Sista paret ut,* Ljus, 1941 (2 eds.), 1943.

—— *Så länge vi leva,* Ljus, 1944.

HILL, GRACE LIVINGSTONE, *Fhebe,* Uppsala: Lindblad, 1922.

—— *Maria,* Uppsala: Lindblad, 1922.

HILLIARD, ALEC R., *Hemligt vapen,* Skoglund, 1943.

HINDUS, MAURICE G., *Att sjunga med änglarna,* Natur och Kultur, 1942.

HOBART, ALICE T., *Ljus i hyddorna,* Hökerberg, 1936 (2 eds.).

HOBSON, LAURA Z., *Icke önskvärd,* Forum, 1944.

HOLMES, WILFRED J., ("Alec Hudson"), *Klart skepp!* Bonnier, 1940.

HOPKINS, NEVIL M., *Mason Brants sällsamma äventyr,* Geber, 1944.

HOUGH, EMERSON, *"The covered wagon."* Bonnier, 1924.

HOWE, HELEN, *Hjärtat har fyra rum,* Bonnier, 1943.

HUESTON, ETHEL, *Prudence,* Skoglund, 1916.

—— *Doris,* Skoglund, 1921.

—— *Prudence's systrar,* Skoglund, 1921.

—— *Swedey,* Skoglund, 1925.

HUGHES, RUPERT, *Vigseln i sovvagnen,* Göteborg: Västra Sverige, 1922.

HUIE, WILLIAM B., *Rena klara stjärnor,* Wahlström & Widstrand, 1945.

HUME, CYRIL, *Den gyllene danserskan,* Schildt, 1929.

HUNTING, HENRY GARDENER, *Mannen som återkallade det förflutna,* Malmö: Norden, 1934.

HURST, FANNIE, *En mannekäng,* Bonnier, 1927.

—— *Femtonöresbasar,* Bonnier, 1931, 1937.

—— *Kärlekens bakgata,* Bonnier, 1933.

—— *Den trygga famnen,* Bonnier, 1937.

HUTTEN, BETSEY BARONESS VON, *Pam,* Wahledow, 1917, 1920.

—— *Mellan far och son,* B. Wahlström, 1919.

—— *Vad det blev av Pam,* Wahledow, 1920.

—— *Glorian,* Wahledow, 1923.

—— *Tommy och Pammy,* Wahledow, 1923.

—— *När kärleken vaknar,* Nutiden, 1927.

IAMS, JACK, *Bord för fyra,* Geber, 1940.

IDELL, ALBERT E., *Den stora sommaren,* Natur och Kultur, 1944.

INGRAM, ELEANOR M., *Dubbelspel,* B. Wahlström, 1918.

IRWIN, WALLACE, *Solens ättlingar,* Norstedt, 1925.

ISHAM, FREDERIC S., *Ett upplöst äktenskap,* Dahlberg, 1918.

—— *Ett vågspel,* Nordiska förlaget, 1919.

JACKSON, CHARLES, *Förspillda dagar,* Norstedt, 1945.

JAMES, HENRY, *Amerikan i Paris,* Natur och Kultur, 1944.

JAMES, WILL, *Vildöga*, Schildt, 1928.

—— *I präriens värld*, Schildt, 1929.

JARRETT, CORA, *Sista natten*, Wahlström & Widstrand, 1934.

JAYNES, CLAIRE, *Jessica lever upp*, Geber, 1944.

JOHNSON, JOSEPHINE W., *Nu i november*, Hökerberg, 1935 (3 eds.).

JOHNSON, OWEN M., *Salamandern*, Geber, 1923.

JOHNSTON, MARY, *Konungens myndling*, B. Wahlström, 1943.

—— *En Virginiens son*, B. Wahlström, 1945.

JORDAN, ELIZABETH G., *Tre år på prov*, Wahlström & Widstrand, 1926.

—— *Svarta fjärilar*, Geber, 1930.

JORDAN, MILDRED A., *En röd ros*, Ljus, 1943.

KAHLER, WOOD, *Bittida i säng*, Schildt, 1929.

KANDEL, ABEN, *När stenarna dansa*, Wahlström & Widstrand, 1945.

KAPSTEIN, ISRAEL J., *Något av en hjälte*, Geber, 1942.

KEELER, HARRY S., *Blonde besten*, Seelig, 1936.

—— *Skottet klockan tio*, Seelig, 1936.

KERR, SOPHIE, *Det blå kuvertet*, Bonnier, 1920.

KEYES, FRANCIS P., *Du har tagit mitt hjärta*, Geber, 1942 (2 eds.).

—— *Guld och glitter*, Geber, 1943.

—— *Karneval i New Orleans*, Geber, 1944, 1945.

KING, BASIL, *Kampen om ett hjärta*, Bonnier, 1918.

KING, MARY P., *Flickan vid oljekällan*, Natur och Kultur, 1942.

KING, RUFUS, *Vem sköt?* Bonnier, 1929.

KIRK, ELLEN W., *Med dammvippa och grytlapp*, Geber, 1931 (6 eds.), 1932 (2 eds.).

KLEIN, CHARLES, *Hon som segrade*, B. Wahlström, 1917.

—— *Kapellmästarn*, Dahlberg, 1919.

KREY, LAURA, *Där stormen dragit fram*, Norstedt, 1939.

KUMMER, FREDERIC A., *Den gröna avgudabilden*, B. Wahlström, 1918, 1924.

—— *Silvermyntets hemlighet*, B. Wahlström, 1920.

—— *De blå signalerna*, Bonnier, 1921.

—— *Hur människan blev jordens herre*, Hökerberg, 1924—1925; Sjöberg, 1926.

KYNE, PETER B., *En karlakarl*, Skoglund, 1923, 1944.

—— *Mexikanen*, Skoglund, 1924 (2 eds.); B. Wahlström, 1936.

—— *Och aldrig mötas de två*, Skoglund, 1925; B. Wahlström, 1937, 1941.

—— *Amerikanen*, Skoglund, 1926.

—— *Det visa hjärtat*, Skoglund, 1927.

—— *Jättarnas dal*, Skoglund, 1928.

—— *Guldfloden*, Skoglund, 1929.

—— *Jim erövraren*, Skoglund, 1930.

—— *Trots allt*, Skoglund. 1931.

—— *Det ärvda guldet*, Skoglund, 1932.

—— *Målet vunnet*, Skoglund, 1933.

—— *Två — en värld,* Skoglund, 1934.

—— *I nöd och lust,* Skoglund, 1935 (2 eds.).

—— *Hjärtat vinner,* Skoglund, 1936.

—— *Starka viljor,* Skoglund, 1937.

—— *Längtans ö,* Skoglund, 1938.

—— *Stramare livsföring,* Skoglund, 1941.

LAING, ALEXANDER K., *Sjöäet,* Norstedt, 1935.

LANDON, HERMAN ("Harry Coverdale"), *De sju okända,* Uppsala: Lindblad, 1930.

LANHAM, EDWIN M., *Det dånar i jorden,* Geber, 1942.

LARSSON, GÖSTA, *Livets nödtorft,* Wahlström & Widstrand, 1934.

—— *Mitt land, farväl!* Wahlström & Widstrand, 1938.

LAWSON, THOMAS W., *Fredagen den 13:de,* Nordiska förlaget, 1917; Vårt hem, 1926; B. Wahlström, 1940.

LEE, HARRY, *Förlorad dag,* Norstedt, 1942.

LE FEUVRE, AMY, *Hilda Törne,* Svenska journalen, 1927.

LEVINGER, ELMA E., *Kanaans frukter,* Aldor, 1932.

LEWIS, ELIZABETH F., *Unge Fu från Kina,* Natur och Kultur, 1934.

—— *Ho-Ming,* Natur och Kultur, 1935.

LEWIS, LANGE, *Mord bland vänner,* Tiden, 1944.

LEWIS, SINCLAIR, *Storgatan,* Thall & Carlsson, 1921—1922; Norstedt, 1927.

—— *Babbitt,* Norstedt, 1923, 1924, 1928.

—— *Vår Mr. Wrenn,* Norstedt, 1924; Saxon & Lindström, 1934.

—— *Falkens bana,* Norstedt, 1925.

—— *Fällan,* Norstedt, 1926; Åhlén & söner, 1933.

—— *Martin Arrowsmith,* Norstedt, 1926, 1927.

—— *Vid ratten,* Norstedt, 1926, 1930.

—— *Jobbet,* Norstedt, 1927, 1930.

—— *Elmer Gantry,* Norstedt, 1928, 1930.

—— *Han som kände Coolidge,* Norstedt, 1928.

—— *Dodsworth,* Norstedt, 1929, 1930.

—— *Blod och bomull,* Federativ, 1930 (3 eds.).

—— *Ann Vickers,* Norstedt, 1933 (3 eds.).

—— *Konstverket,* Norstedt, 1934; Saxon & Lindström, 1942.

—— *Sånt händer inte här,* Norstedt, 1936.

—— *Vi leker kung och andra historier,* Norstedt, 1937.

—— *Vanartiga föräldrar,* Norstedt, 1938.

—— *Bethel Merriday,* Norstedt, 1941.

—— *Gideon Planish,* Norstedt, 1945.

LEWISOHN, LUDWIG, *Den slutna kretsen,* Norstedt, 1930.

—— *Makarna Crump,* Norstedt, 1932.

—— *Stephen Escott,* Norstedt, 1933.

—— *Dick Beldens altare,* Norstedt, 1935.

—— *Försoningens dag,* Norstedt, 1937.

—— *Hjärtat och världen,* Norstedt, 1940.

LINCOLN, JOSEPH C., *En hederspamp,* Bohlin, 1925.

—— *Kapten Eri,* Bohlin, 1926.

LOFTING, HUGH, *Doktor Doolittles underbara resor,* Schildt, 1928.

—— *Doktor Doolittles postkontor,* Schildt, 1929.

LONDON, JACK, *Skriet från vildmarken,* Bohlin, 1907, 1909, 1910, 1911, 1913, 1916, 1920, 1924, 1925; Uppsala: Lindblad, 1916; Nordiska förlaget, 1917; Saxon & Lindström, 1935; Malmö: Norden, 1940; *När vildmarken kallar,* Holmquist, 1914, 1919; Nutiden, 1919.

—— *Vargens son,* Bohlin, 1907, 1909, 1912, 1918, 1923, 1926; B. Wahlström, 1912; Dahlberg, 1919; Romanbiblioteket, 1922.

—— *Varghunden,* Bohlin, 1908, 1910, 1911, 1912, 1916, 1917, 1920, 1925; Uppsala: Lindblad, 1917, B. Wahlström, 1917; Malmö: Norden, 1940; *Vita huggtanden,* Holmquist, 1917, 1918 (3 eds.).

—— *Före Adam,* Bohlin, 1909 (2 eds.), 1915, 1916, 1917 (2 eds.), 1918, 1924; Holmquist, 1918; Dahlberg, 1919; Åhlén & Åkerlund, 1921; Romanbiblioteket, 1922.

—— *Varg-Larsen,* Bohlin, 1909 (2 eds.), 1910, 1914, 1918, 1922, 1926; B. Wahlström, 1914; Dahlberg, 1919; Romanbiblioteket, 1922; Malmö: Norden, 1940; *Havsvargen,* Holmquist, 1917.

—— *Avgrundens folk,* Bohlin, 1910, 1913 (2 eds.), 1916, 1917, 1919, 1925; Nordiska förlaget, 1913; Dahlberg, 1919; Holmquist, 1919; Romanbiblioteket, 1922; Bonnier, 1945.

—— *För mycket guld och andra berättelser från Klondyke,* Bohlin, 1910, 1917, 1918 (2 eds.), 1925; B. Wahlström, 1914; Dahlberg, 1919; Romanbiblioteket, 1922.

—— *På kryssning med Blixten,* Bille, 1910; Holmquist, 1913; B. Wahlström, 1920; *På kryss med Blixten,* Nordiska förlaget, 1914; Bohlin, 1917, 1921, 1924; Bonnier, 1917; B. Wahlström, 1945.

—— *Hans fäders Gud och andra berättelser från Klondyke,* Bohlin, 1911, 1916, 1917, 1918, 1923, 1926; Holmquist, 1911, 1913, 1918; Dahlberg, 1919; Romanbiblioteket, 1922.

—— *Nordlandets dotter,* Bohlin, 1911, 1916, 1917, 1918 (2 eds.), 1924, 1926; Dahlberg, 1919; Romanbiblioteket, 1923; *Snöviddernas dotter,* Holmquist, 1913, 1917, 1919.

—— *På långfärd med Snark,* Bohlin, 1911, 1917, 1919, 1925.

—— *Hedningen och andra berättelser från Söderhafsöarna,* Bohlin, 1912, 1917, 1919, 1925.

—— *Järnhälen,* Bohlin, 1912, 1916, 1918, 1920 (2 eds.), 1926; Åhlén & Åkerlund, 1919; Holmquist, 1919.

—— *Martin Eden,* Bohlin, 1912, 1915, 1918, 1920, 1925.

—— *Kärlek till livet,* Bohlin, 1913, 1916, 1917, 1922, 1925; Holmquist, 1918, 1920; Dahlberg, 1919; Romanbiblioteket, 1922; B. Wahlström, 1944.

—— *Köldens barn,* Holmquist, 1913 (2 eds.), 1917; Bohlin, 1918, 1922, 1926.
—— *Kungen av Klondyke,* Bohlin, 1913 (2 eds.), 1917, 1920, 1925.
—— *Patrullbåten,* Holmquist, 1913, 1917, 1919.
—— *John Finkelman,* Bohlin, 1914, 1915, 1919, 1923; *Kung Alkohol eller en drinkares minnen,* Nutiden, 1917.
—— *Måndalen,* Bohlin, 1914, 1919, 1924, 1926.
—— *Jees Ucks historia och andra berättelser,* Holmquist, 1914, 1919 (2 eds.).
—— *Månansiktet och andra berättelser,* Holmquist, 1914 (2 eds.), 1918; Bohlin, 1918, 1925, 1927; Dahlberg, 1919; Romanbiblioteket, 1922.
—— *Strejkbrytaren,* Göteborg: John Andersson, 1914.
—— *All världens fiende med flera berättelser,* Bohlin, 1915, 1918, 1925.
—— *Myteriet på "Helsingör"* Bohlin, 1915, 1916, 1919, 1925.
—— *Söderhavsberättelser,* Bohlin, 1915, 1919, 1925.
—— *Äventyr,* Bohlin, 1916, 1918 (2 eds.), 1925; Vårt hem, 1925.
—— *För sista gången,* Holmquist, 1916 (2 eds.).
—— *På vakt,* B. Wahlström, 1916.
—— *Tvångströjan,* Bohlin, 1916, 1920, 1926.
—— *Vagabondlif,* Bohlin, 1916, 1917, 1918, 1925; Holmquist, 1918 (2 eds.), 1919; Dahlberg, 1919; Romanbiblioteket, 1922; *På luffen,* Nordiska förlaget, 1918.
—— *Afgrundsdjuret,* Bohlin, 1917, 1920, 1926.
—— *En nordens odyssé,* Holmquist, 1917, 1919.
—— *Jerry,* Bohlin, 1917, 1926; Vårt hem, 1926.
—— *Planchette,* Holmquist, 1917, 1919.
—— *Samlade skrifter,* Bohlin, vols. I—XXXI, 1917—1920; vol. XXXII, 1922; vol. XI *(Varg-Larsen),* 2nd. edition, 1922.
—— *En solens son,* Bohlin, 1918, 1920, 1926; B. Wahlström, 1936.
—— *Kärlekens väsen,* Bohlin, 1918, 1922, 1926.
—— *Revolution,* Karlstad: Klasskampens förlag, 1918.
—— *Röda pesten,* Bohlin, 1918, 1927.
—— *Solguld och andra berättelser,* Bohlin, 1918, 1922.
—— *Klasskamp, Revolution och andra essayer,* Bohlin, 1919, 1927; *Klasskampen,* Holmquist 1919.
—— *Michael, Jerrys bror,* Bohlin, 1919.
—— *Nigger Bellew,* Bohlin, 1919, 1926.
—— *Vägen,* Nutiden, 1919.
—— *Den lilla damen i det stora huset,* Bohlin, 1920.
—— *Den röde guden, Spelet,* Bohlin, 1920.
—— *Glödande kol och andra noveller, Efterskörd,* Bohlin, 1920.
—— *Kvinnofejd, Stöld, Ollonodlaren,* Bohlin, 1920.
—— *När gudarna skratta och andra historier, Nattens barn och andra berättelser,* Bohlin, 1920.
—— *Hawaji-noveller,* Bohlin, 1922, 1927.

—— *Tre hjärtan*, Bohlin, 1922.

—— *Valda skrifter*, Malmö: Svenska förlagshuset, vols. I—II, 1925; vols. III—XV, 1926.

—— *Valda skrifter*, Malmö: Världslitteraturen, vols. I—XX, 1926—1927.

—— *Valda arbeten*, B. Wahlström, vols. I—XV, 1929; paper bound edition, 1930.

—— *Skrifter*, Malmö: [Malmö konsttryckanstalt], vols. I—XVI, 1939—1940 (sold by mail).

LONDON, JACK, and ANNA STRUNSKY, *Kärlekens problem*, B. Wahlström, 1914.

LONG, WILLIAM J., *Vildmarksseder*, Geber, 1914, 1917, 1921.

—— *I vildmarkens hägn*, Geber, 1915, 1919, 1926.

—— *På nordliga stigar*, Geber, vol. I, 1916 (2 eds.), 1922; vol. II, 1917 (2 eds.), 1921.

—— *Ur djurens liv*, Geber, 1918 (3 eds.), 1922.

—— *Vad skogen lär*, Geber, vol. I, 1912, 1915, 1919; vol. II, 1912, 1916, 1920.

—— *Skogens hemligheter*, Geber, 1919, 1923.

—— *Hur djuren tala*, Geber, 1920 (3 eds.), 1926.

—— *Skogarnas lustspel*, Geber, 1921 (2 eds.).

—— *Björnens lillebror*, Geber, 1922.

—— *Moder jord*, Geber, 1924 (2 eds.).

LOOMIS, FREDERIC, *Bandet som förenar*, Sohlman, 1944.

LOOS, ANITA, *Herrar tycker bäst om blondiner*, Bonnier, 1926 (2 eds.).

—— *... men dom gifter sig med brunetter*, Bonnier, 1928.

LYNCH, GERTRUDE, *Med lyftad vinge*, B. Wahlström, 1916.

LYTLE, ANDREW N., *Värdshuset Månen*, Sohlman, 1943.

McCLOY, HELEN, *Sanningen som dödar*, Skoglund, 1942.

—— *Hallå, vem är det?* Skoglund, 1944.

—— *Vad ville han?* Skoglund, 1944.

—— *Dödsdansen*, Skoglund, 1945.

McCLURE, ROBERT E., *Harry Pickering*, B. Wahlström, 1939.

McCULLERS, CARSON, *Hjärtat jagar allena*, Geber, 1941 (2 eds.).

—— *Spegling i ett gyllne öga*, Geber, 1943.

McCUTCHEON, GEORGE B., *Graustark*, Göteborg: Västra Sverige, 1917.

—— *Lady Pen's snedsprång*, B. Wahlström, 1923.

MACDONALD, JESSICA NORTH, *Gryning över landet*, Uppsala: Lindblad, 1943.

McEVOY, JOSEPH P., *Dixie dansar*, Schildt, 1929.

MACGRATH, HAROLD, *Mannen på kuskbocken*, Bonnier, 1918; Nordiska förlaget, 1918.

—— *Den mystiska ön*, Bonnier, 1920.

—— *Papegoja & Co.*, Bonnier, 1920.

MACHARG, WILLIAM, and EDWIN BALMER, *Den blinde mannens ögon*, Geber, 1918.

—— *Luther Trants bedrifter*, Geber 1919.

—— *En duell i mörkret*, Geber, 1920.

—— *Indiantrummans hemlighet*, Geber, 1921.

McIntyre, John T., *Porträttets hemlighet*, B. Wahlström, 1916.

McKay, Allis, *Flickan vid floden*, Bonnier, 1944.

Macvane, Edith, *På jakt efter en miljonär*, Nordiska förlaget, 1918.

Magruder, Julia, *Hennes misstag*, Nordiska förlaget, 1918.

Major, Charles, *Mary Tudor och Charles Brandon*, Fahlcrantz, 1925.

Maltz, Albert, *Korset och pilen*, Ljus, 1945.

Marks, Percy, *Martha*, Geber, 1928.

—— *Från höst till höst*, Tiden, 1943.

Marquand, John P., *Den svarta lasten*, Bonnier, 1926.

—— *Boston*, Hökerberg, 1938.

—— *Fint folk*, Norstedt, 1940.

—— *En viss Mr. Pulham*, Norstedt, 1942.

—— *Ännu en tid*, Norstedt, 1944.

—— *Rapsodi i gult*, Norstedt, 1945.

Marshall, Edison, *Det stora äventyret*, Ljus, 1944.

—— *Benjamin äventyraren*, Ljus, 1945.

Martyn, Wyndham, *Anthony Trent, gentlemannatjuv*, Schildt, 1931.

—— *Mr. Devlin, Trents överman*, Schildt, 1931.

—— *Mr. Trent möter Devlin*, Schildt, 1931.

Mason, Caroline A., *En högre väg, eller Kärlekens seger*, B. M:s bokförlag, 1925.

Mason, F. Van Wyck, *Affären Guatecata*, Göteborg: Romanförlaget, 1935.

—— *Tre hamnar*, Hökerberg, 1939.

—— *Frihetsskeppet*, Rabén & Sjögren, 1944.

Medearis, Mary, *Arvet och drömmen*, Ljus, 1943.

Meloney, William B., *Flykt mot solen*, Fritze, 1942.

Melville, Herman, *Moby Dick eller den vita valen*, Ljus, 1943.

Michelson, Miriam, *Jessie Incells kärlek*, Åhlén & Åkerlund, 1920.

Miller, Caroline, *I ditt anletes svett*, Bonnier, 1935.

Mirza, Youël, *Jalal är vår hövding*, Fahlcrantz & Gumælius, 1941.

Mitchell, John ("John Chester"), *Spiritistdamen*, Jönköping: Strömberg & Åhlén, 1922.

Mitchell, John Ames, *Gud Amor*, Nordiska förlaget, 1919.

—— *Den unge rajahn*, Holmquist, 1923.

Mitchell, Margaret, *Borta med vinden*, Medén, 1937 (3 eds.), 1938 (3 eds.), 1940.

Morley, Christopher, *Människobarn*, Geber, 1926.

—— *Kitty Foyle*, Medén, 1940.

Morris, Ira V., *Frihetens gata*, Skoglund, 1945.

Mowery, William B., *Vildmarkens sång*, B. Wahlström, 1936.

—— *Den gyllene floden*, B. Wahlström, 1937.

—— *En nordlandets son*, B. Wahlström, 1937.

—— *Den förbjudna dalen*, B. Wahlström, 1939.

—— *Vildmarkens rop*, B. Wahlström, 1940.

—— *Silverhöken*, B. Wahlström, 1943.

—— *Spåret över bergen*, B. Wahlström, 1943.

—— *Flickan i Paradisdalen*, B. Wahlström, 1945.

MUNDY, TALBOT, *Aum, Ahbordalens hemlighet*, Bonnier, 1926.

—— *Mysteriet vid Charles Street*, Göteborg: Romanförlaget, 1935.

MYERS, JOHN M., *Harpan och svärdet*, Tiden, 1943.

—— *Fattiga riddare*, Tiden, 1944.

NATHAN, ROBERT, *Tidig vår*, Skoglund, 1941.

—— *Tillsammans — vidare*, Steinsvik, 1944.

NEILSON, ELISABETH, *Oförgätligt ler mitt hem*, Ljus, 1941.

NICHOLSON, MEREDITH, *Huset med de tusen ljusen*, Bonnier, 1917.

NORDHOFF, CHARLES, *Vraket i lagunen*, Bonnier, 1936.

—— *Pärllagunen*, Bonnier, 1938.

NORDHOFF, CHARLES, and JAMES N. HALL, *Myteri!* Bonnier, 1934, 1936 (2 eds.);
  Myteriet på Bounty, Bonnier, 1941.

—— *Kamp mot sjön*, Bonnier, 1935, 1936.

—— *Myteristernas ö*, Bonnier, 1936.

—— *Orkan över Söderhavet*, Bonnier, 1938, 1940.

—— *Den mörka floden*, Bonnier, 1939.

—— *Botany Bay*, Bonnier, 1942, 1945.

—— *Män utan fosterland*, Bonnier, 1943.

NORRIS, FRANK, *En kvinnas makt*, Holmquist, 1917, 1926.

—— *Ungdomskärlek*, Nutiden, 1918; Saxon & Lindström, 1933.

—— *Oceanens dotter*, Åhlén & Åkerlund, 1925.

NORRIS, KATHLEEN, *Rakels hjärta*, Fritze, 1917; *Rakels äktenskap*, Åhlén & Åkerlund, 1922.

—— *Ett hjärtas eldprov*, Vårt hem, 1922.

—— *På kärlekens vägar*, Åhlén & Åkerlund, 1923.

—— *Lucrezia Lombard*, Åhlén & Åkerlund, 1924.

—— *Norma*, Åhlén & Åkerlund, 1924.

—— *Två systrar*, Åhlén & Åkerlund, 1925, 1926.

—— *Små skepp*, Åhlén & Åkerlund, 1926.

—— *Clem Riordans lycka*, Åhlén & Åkerlund, 1927.

—— *Hemligheten med Gabrielle*, Åhlén & Åkerlund, 1933.

O'CONNOR, MARY P., *Ett hemlighetsfullt mord*, B. Wahlström, 1916, 1924.

OPPENHEIM, JAMES, *Doktor Rast*, Åhlén & Åkerlund, 1921.

OSBOURNE, LLOYD, *Bilkurtis*, B. Wahlström, 1917, 1927.

OSTENSO, MARTHA, *Vildgäss*, Bonnier, 1926.

—— *Den mörka gryningen*, Bonnier, 1927.

OSTRANDER, ISABEL E., *Flickan med ärret*, Bonnier, 1925.

—— *De tjugosex ledtrådarna*, Bonnier, 1926.

—— *Den andra kulan*, Vårt hem, 1928.

—— *Intrigernas ö*, Bonnier, 1928.

—— *Den grå handsken*, Bonnier, 1929.

OURSLER, FULTON, *En drömmare*, Geber, 1929.

PACKARD, FRANK L., *Höken*, B. Wahlström, 1919, 1926.

—— *Jimmie Dale*, Bonnier, 1924.

—— *Damen i svart*, Bonnier, 1926.

PALEN, LEWIS S., *Svarta havets fasa*, Uppsala: Lindblad, 1927.

PARKER, DOROTHY, *Efter kärlekens nöjen*, Wahlström & Widstrand, 1945.

PARRISH, ANNE, *Den ståndaktige ungkarlen*, Bonnier, 1926.

PAUL, ELLIOT H., *Den trånga gatan*, Wahlström & Widstrand, 1943.

PECK, GEORGE W., *Tjuvpojkstreck*, Bonnier, 1917.

PENTECOST, HUGH, *Överstämplad med rött*, Ljus, 1944.

PEPLE, EDWARD H., *Vildkatten*, Nordiska förlaget, 1917.

—— *De stulna juvelerna*, Holmquist, 1922.

PHILLIPS, DAVID G., *Susan Lenox*, Hökerberg, 1924.

—— *Rika män och deras kvinnor*, Hökerberg, 1925.

—— *Priset hon betalade*, Hökerberg, 1926.

—— *Rika män och deras barn*, Hökerberg, 1927.

—— *Hon och jag*, Hökerberg, 1928.

—— *Högt spel*, Hökerberg, 1929.

—— *En segrare*, Hökerberg, 1930.

—— *Hjärtat som hungrar*, Hökerberg, 1931.

—— *Hennes vilja*, Hökerberg, 1932.

—— *Nya hustrur*, Hökerberg, 1933.

—— *En lycksökare*, Hökerberg, 1934.

POE, EDGAR A., *Hemlighetsfulla och fantastiska historier*, Björck & Börjesson, 1916.

—— *Bandstumpen*, Holmquist, 1917.

—— *Myteriet på briggen Späckhuggaren*, Nordiska förlaget, 1918.

—— *Guldbaggen och andra noveller*, Bonnier, 1922.

—— *Morden på Rue de la Morgue och andra underliga historier*, Bonnier, 1922.

—— *Sällsamma historier*, Björck & Börjesson, 1922.

—— *Sällsamma historier*, Schildt, 1929.

—— *Sällsamma historier*, Malmö: Världslitteraturen, 1931.

—— *Sällsamma berättelser*, Saxon & Lindström, 1935.

—— *Sällsamma historier*, Kungsholmens bokhandel, 1938.

POLONSKY, ABRAHAM, *Fientligt hav*, Ljus, 1944.

POPE, EDITH, *Skuggor över Florida*, Norstedt, 1945.

PORTER, ELEANOR H., *"Bara David"* Bonnier, 1916.

—— *Violinvirtuosen*, Nordiska förlaget, 1917.

—— *Pollyanna*, Uppsala: Lindblad, 1918, 1920 (2 eds.).

—— *Vägen till förståelse*, Fritze, 1918.

—— *Åh, pengar, pengar!* Fritze, 1919.

—— *Pollyanna växer upp,* Uppsala: Lindblad, 1919 (2 eds.).

PORTER, WILLIAM S. ("O. Henry"), *De fyra miljonerna,* Nutiden, 1919.

—— *Prima patenterade samveten,* Dahlberg, 1919.

—— *Valda noveller,* Fahlcrantz, 1919.

—— *Ödets vägar och andra berättelser,* Fahlcrantz, 1920.

—— *Stadens stämma och andra berättelser,* Göteborg: Pehrssons förlag, 1929; Natur och Kultur, 1945.

POST, MELVILLE D., *Sir Henrys bedrifter,* Geber, 1927.

POTTER, DAVID, *Armbandet,* Nordiska förlaget, 1918.

PRATT, THEODORE, *Fem män och en kvinna,* Geber, 1943.

PROKOSCH, FREDERIC, *Asiater,* Tiden, 1937 (2 eds.).

—— *De sju som flydde,* Tiden, 1938 (2 eds.).

—— *Skyar över Europa,* Tiden, 1942.

—— *Konspiratörer,* Tiden, 1943.

—— *Åskans tid,* Tiden, 1945.

PROPPER, MILTON M., *Snälltåget 7.45,* Tiden, 1931; B. Wahlström, 1944.

—— *Rum nr 822,* Tiden, 1932.

—— *Tunnelgåtan,* B. Wahlström, 1933.

—— *Mordgåtan i studentorden,* B. Wahlström, 1934.

PROUTY, OLIVE H., *Femte hjulet,* Bonnier, 1918.

—— *Mor och dotter,* Bonnier, 1925.

—— *Lisa Vale,* Norstedt, 1939.

—— *Under nya stjärnor,* Ljus, 1943.

"QUEEN, ELLERY," *Konsthandlarens kista,* Bonnier, 1933, 1940.

—— *X-tragedien,* Geber, 1933.

—— *Draksådden,* Bonnier, 1937.

—— *Mandarinmysteriet,* Bonnier, 1938.

—— *Den stängda dörren,* Bonnier, 1940.

—— *Mr Queen har otur,* Bonnier, 1943.

"QUEEN, ELLERY, JR.," *Sköldpaddsmysteriet,* Ljus, 1945.

RAWLINGS, MARJORIE K., *Hjortkalven,* Bonnier, 1940.

—— *I hjortkalvens marker,* Bonnier, 1943.

REEVE, ARTHUR B., *Den gula demonen,* B. Wahlström, 1918, 1926.

—— *Den knutna handen,* B. Wahlström, 1918, 1926, 1935.

—— *Craig Kennedys triumf,* B, Wahlström, 1919, 1926.

—— *Äventyrskan,* Vårt hem, 1928.

—— *Den ljudlösa kulan,* B. Wahlström, 1934.

—— *Craig Kennedy rycker in,* Göteborg: Romanförlaget, 1935.

—— *Craig Kennedys största affär,* Göteborg: Romanförlaget, 1935.

REID, MAYNE, *Nybyggarliv i vilda västern,* Holmquist, 1920, 1931.

REILLY, HELEN, *Fråga de döda,* Bonnier, 1941.

—— *Sörjd på en sondag,* Bonnier, 1942.

RICE, ELMER, *Resan till Puerilien,* Wahlström & Widstrand, 1931.

—— *Världsstad,* Bonnier, 1938.

RICHMOND, GRACE S., *Doktorns patienter,* Geber, 1923, 1944.

RINEHART, MARY R., *"K"* Bonnier, 1916, 1919.

—— *Ett äventyr på en lustjakt,* Dahlberg, 1918.

—— *Sjustjärnegatan,* Bonnier, 1918.

—— *Den levande döda,* Dahlberg, 1919.

—— *Spiral trappan,* Åhlén & Åkerlund, 1920, 1927; Saxon & Lindström, 1940.

—— *Den röda lampan,* Bonnier, 1927.

—— *Nomadernas land,* Bonnier, 1927.

—— *Döden har bråttom,* Bonnier, 1936.

—— *Det spökar hos Mrs. Fairbanks,* Bonnier, 1944.

ROBERTS, EDITH K., *Gifta,* Wahlström & Widstrand, 1942.

ROBERTS, ELIZABETH M., *Prövotider,* Geber, 1929.

—— *De vida fälten,* Geber, 1931.

ROBERTS, KENNETH L., *Arundel,* Bonnier, 1939.

—— *Oliver Wiswell,* Bonnier, 1941.

—— *Nordvästpassagen,* Bonnier, 1938, 1939, 1942.

—— *Slödder i vapen,* Bonnier, 1944, 1945.

ROCHE, ARTHUR S., *Var är kvinnan?* Geber, 1925.

ROHLFS, ANNA GREEN, *Briljantringen,* B. Wahlström, 1916.

—— *En trasslig härva,* B. Wahlström, 1916.

—— *Hattnålen,* B. Wahlström, 1916.

—— *Jeffery-Moore mysteriet,* B. Wahlström, 1916.

—— *Damen i alkoven,* Bonnier, 1917; B. Wahlström, 1917, 1924, 1935.

—— *Den försvunna bruden,* B. Wahlström, 1917.

—— *Ett hemlighetsfullt uppdrag,* Holmquist, 1917, 1925.

—— *Mordet vid femte avenyn,* B. Wahlström, 1917, 1925.

—— *Homewoodmysteriet,* B. Wahlström, 1919.

—— *Purpurorkidéen,* B. Wahlström, 1923.

ROTHERMELL, FRED, *Tornet som lutade,* Skoglund, 1935.

RUSSELL, JOHN, *Där vägarna bli osäkra,* Geber, 1926.

—— *Platser som Gud glömde,* Geber, 1928.

RYAN, MARAH ELLIS, *Genesee Jack,* Åhlén & Åkerlund, 1920.

ST. JOHN, ROBERT, *Med kriget i hälarna,* Tiden, 1944.

SANTAYANA, GEORGE, *Den siste puritanen,* Natur och Kultur, 1936.

SAROYAN, WILLIAM, *Jag heter Aram,* Bonnier, 1944.

SAVAGE, RICHARD H., *Min hustru för en vecka,* Svenska andelsförlaget, 1927; *Min officiella hustru,* Malmö: Union, 1929; B. Wahlström, 1939.

SAXTON, MARK, *Mörkt spel,* Norstedt, 1944.

SCHULBERG, BUDD, *Varför springer Sammy?* Skoglund, 1942.

SCOGGINS, CHARLES E., *Mahogny,* Wahlström & Widstrand, 1939.

—— *Gryningens hus,* Wahlström & Widstrand, 1941.

—— *Pampa Joe,* Wahlström & Widstrand, 1943.

SCOTT, REGINALD T. M., *Mannen som aldrig dog,* Wahlström & Widstrand, 1931.

SEAWELL, MOLLY E. ("Foxcroft Davis"), *Senator Clavering och hans dotter,* Nordiska förlaget, 1922.

SEDGWICK, ANNE D., *En liten fransk flicka,* Geber, 1926 (2 eds.).

—— *Det befriade hjärtat,* Geber, 1931.

—— *Philippa,* Geber, 1932.

SETON, ANYA, *Det hände på Dragonwyck,* B. Wahlström, 1945.

SHEEAN, VINCENT, *Luisa Sanfelice,* Medén, 1936.

—— *Anno 1745,* Medén, 1938.

—— *I elfte timmen,* Wahlström & Widstrand, 1939.

—— *Vildmarkens fågel,* Norstedt, 1943.

SHELDON, CHARLES M., *I hans fotspår eller "vad skulle Jesus göra?"* Harrier, 1942.

SHELLABARGER, SAMUEL, *Erövraren från Kastilien,* Bonnier, 1945.

SHIBER, ETTA, *Under jorden i Paris,* Bonnier, 1944.

SIMS, MARIAN M., *Är detta frihet?* Norstedt, 1938.

—— *P. M. för en äkta man,* Fritze, 1944.

SINCLAIR, UPTON, *Vildmarken,* Excelsior, 1906; Nordiska förlaget, 1906; Björck & Börjesson, 1906 (3 eds.); Holmström, 1925, 1928; Bonnier, 1945.

—— *Börsbaronen,* Silen, 1906; B. Wahlström, 1913; Holmström, 1924, 1928.

—— *Industrirepubliken eller Amerika om tio år,* Björck & Börjesson, 1909.

—— *Ett problem,* Nordiska förlaget, 1911; *Samuel sökaren,* Holmström, 1925, 1928.

—— *Kung Kol,* Holmström, 1917, 1923, 1927, 1941.

—— *Jimmie Higgins,* Holmström, 1919 (2 eds.), 1924, 1929.

—— *Under religionens täckmantel,* Holmström, 1920—1921, 1926, 1928.

—— *Hundra procent,* Holmström, 1921, 1927.

—— *Man kallar mig timmerman,* Holmström, 1922 (2 eds.), 1926.

—— *Det tusenåriga riket,* Holmström, 1924 (2 eds.), 1928.

—— *Olja,* Holmström, 1926 (2 eds.), 1928.

—— *Brev till Judd,* Holmström, 1927.

—— *Bunny Ross,* Holmström, 1927.

—— *Kärlekens pilgrimsfärd,* Holmström, 1927.

—— *Wall street,* Holmström, 1927.

—— *Boston,* Holmström, 1928—1929.

—— *Gyllene länkar,* Holmström, 1928.

—— *Manassas,* Holmström, 1929.

—— *Så gör man dollars,* Holmström, 1931.

—— *Våta paraden,* Holmström, 1934.

—— *Våra liv för Spanien,* Holmström, 1937 (2 eds.).

—— *Bilkungen,* Holmström, 1938.

—— *Kämpande stål,* Holmström, 1939.

—— *De sådde vind ...,* Holmström, 1941.

—— *Mellan två världar,* Holmström, 1942, 1943 (2 eds.).

—— *Drakens tänder,* Holmström, 1943.

—— *Förtappelsens väg,* Holmström, 1944.

—— *Presidentens agent,* Holmström, 1945.

SLAUGHTER, FRANK G., *Livet skall räddas,* Ljus, 1943.

—— *Vi tjäna livet,* Ljus, 1944.

—— *För livets skull,* Ljus, 1945.

SMEDLEY, AGNES, *Bara en kvinna,* Tiden, 1931.

—— *Kina! Kina!* Tiden, 1934.

SMITH, BETTY, *Det växte ett träd i Brooklyn,* Wahlström & Widstrand, 1944.

SMITH, HARRIET L., *Pollyanna som gift,* Uppsala: Lindblad, 1929 (2 eds.).

—— *Pollyannas juveler,* Uppsala, 1930 (2 eds.).

SMITH, HOMER W., *Lungfisken,* Geber, 1932.

SMITH, LILLIAN E., *Sällsam frukt,* Bonnier, 1945.

SMITTER, WESSEL, *Fritt Detroit,* Steinsvik, 1944.

—— *Nya tag,* Steinsvik, 1945.

STEELE, JACK, *En lånad äkta man,* B. Wahlström, 1917.

STEINBECK, JOHN E., *Riddarna kring Dannys bord,* Bonnier, 1938; Forum, 1944.

—— *Möss och människor,* Bonnier, 1939.

—— *Vredens druvor,* Bonnier, 1940, 1941, 1944, 1945.

—— *Månen har gått ned,* Bonnier, 1942, 1943.

—— *Den långa dalen,* Bonnier, 1943.

—— *Det stora kalaset,* Bonnier, 1945.

STEPHENS, ROBERT N., *Vägen till Paris,* Ocean, 1945.

STEVENSON, BURTON E., *På falskt pass,* Bonnier, 1917.

—— *Den behandskade handen,* Dahlberg, 1919.

—— *En kung i Babylon,* Geber, 1919.

—— *Den osynlige,* Åhlén & Åkerlund, 1921.

—— *Holladay-målet,* B. Wahlström, 1936; *Fallet Holladay,* B. Wahlström, 1943.

STEWART, GEORGE R., *Med dig till världens ände,* Medén, 1942.

—— *Oväder,* Ljus, 1942.

STONE, GRACE Z. ("Ethel Vance"), *Repressalier,* Bonnier, 1944.

STONE, IRVING, *Han som älskade livet,* Natur och Kultur, 1935 (2 eds.), 1936, 1937, 1938, 1942.

—— *Falskt vittnesbörd,* Wahlström & Widstrand, 1941.

—— *Odödlig kvinna,* Natur och Kultur, 1945.

STONG, PHILIP D., *Lyckans karusell,* Bonnier, 1933.

STOUT, REX, *Det röda skrinet,* Norstedt, 1939.

—— *Mord bland mästerkockar,* Norstedt, 1939.

—— *Rädda herrars klubb,* Norstedt, 1939.

—— *Caesar är död,* Norstedt, 1940.

—— *Fer-de-lance,* Norstedt, 1940.

STOWE, HARRIET B., *Han kommer i morgon*, Fosterlandsstiftelsen, 1919, 1935.

—— *Onkel Toms stuga*, Fosterlandsstiftelsen, 1921, 1937; Pallas, 1925; Saxon & Lindström, 1929; Malmö: Baltiska förlaget, 1929; Ardor, 1931, 1933, 1936, 1940, 1942, 1945; Harrier, 1945.

STREET, JAMES H., *Ödet ledde deras steg*, Ljus, 1945.

STRIBLING, THOMAS S., *Lejonets hjärta*, Åhlén & Åkerlund, 1925.

STUART, JESSE H., *Hurra för soldat Tussie!* Ljus, 1945.

STUART, WARREN, *Svärdet och nätet*, Bonnier, 1942.

STURE-VASA, MARY O'HARA, *Hans vän Piken*, Ljus, 1942.

—— *Åskmolnet*, Ljus, 1944, 1945.

SUCKOW, RUTH, *Fergusons*, Norstedt, 1936.

TARKINGTON, BOOTH, *Flirt*, Göteborg: Västra Sverige, 1916.

—— *Penrod*, Åhlén & Åkerlund, 1918.

—— *De magnifika Ambersons*, Fahlcrantz, 1919.

—— *Mannen från Indiana*, Holmquist, 1923, 1928.

—— *En familjeflicka*, Wahlström & Widstrand, 1925.

—— *Två män om ett namn*, Vårt hem, 1926.

—— *Sjutton år*, Wahlström & Widstrand, 1927.

—— *En penningfurste*, Norstedt, 1928.

TERHUNE, ALBERT P., *Det blå husets hemlighet*, Holmquist, 1916.

—— *"Lad"*, Bonnier, 1922; *Vår egen hund*, Åhlén & Åkerlund, 1933.

—— *Mera om Lad*, [n.p.], 1925.

—— *Svarte Cesars klan*, Geber, 1926.

—— *Treve*, Bonnier, 1930.

—— *Hunden Ruffs bravader*, Bonnier, 1935.

—— *Ryktbara hundar*, Lindqvist, 1938.

THAYER, TIFFANY E., *Tretton kvinnor*, Aldor, 1932.

THOMAS, LOWELL, *Lauterbach från Kinesiska sjön*, Schildt, 1933.

TILLETT, DOROTHY S. ("John Stephen Strange"), *Mördaren beklagar sorgen*, Norstedt, 1944.

TRUAX, RHODA, *En läkaredynasti*, Rabén & Sjögren, 1943.

TRUMBULL, ROBERT O., *Flotten*, Bonnier, 1943.

TULLY, JIM, *Rälsens riddare*, Union, 1926.

TUTTLE, MARGARETTA, *Den gyllne reflexen*, Åhlén & Åkerlund, 1924.

VANCE, LOUIS J., *Damen i grått*, B. Wahlström, 1917.

—— *Portlandsjuvelerna*, Malmö: Svenska konstförlaget, 1917.

—— *Svarta handväskan*, B. Wahlström, 1919.

—— *På fritid*, Hökerberg, 1929.

VANDERCOOK, JOHN W., *Hans svarta majestät*, Natur och Kultur, 1928.

VAN VECHTEN, CARL, *Negrernas himmelrike*, Almqvist & Wiksell, 1927.

—— *En fånge i Hollywood*, Schildt, 1929.

VERRILL, ALPHEUS H., *Radiodetektiverna*, Åhlén & Åkerlund, 1923.

WADDELL, CHARLES CAREY, *Rubinhalsbandet,* B. Wahlström, 1917, 1926.
—— *Den stora juvelstölden,* B. Wahlström, 1923.
WAGNALLS, MABEL, *Farornas palats,* Nordiska förlaget, 1919.
WALKER, MILDRED, *De stora bryggarhästarna,* Natur och Kultur, 1941.
—— *När vetet mognar,* Natur och Kultur, 1944.
WALKER, STANLEY, *Rena galenskapen,* Hökerberg, 1936.
WALLACE, LEWIS, *Ben Hur,* Uppsala: Almqvist & Wiksell, 1924, 1927; Uppsala: Lindblad, 1924; Malmö: Baltiska förlaget, 1928, Malmö: Norden, 1932; Lindqvist, 1939.
WALLER, MARY E., *En vrå bland bergen,* Uppsala: Lindblad, 1927.
WARD, CHRISTOPHER L., *Berättelsen om de sällsamma äventyr, som upplevdes av Jonathan Drew,* Norstedt, 1934.
—— *Den oförbätterlige vagabonden,* Norstedt, 1935.
WARREN, LELLA, *Grundstenen,* Forum, 1944.
WATKIN, LAWRENCE, *Vill kärlek ta råd av en vis?* Hökerberg, 1944.
WEAVER, JOHN V. A., *Hennes riddare kommer,* Chelius, 1931.
WEBSTER, HENRY K., *Den viskande mannen,* B. Wahlström, 1917, 1934.
—— *Familjen Corbett,* Hökerberg, 1920.
—— *Joseph Greer och hans dotter,* Hökerberg, 1925.
—— *Mary Wollaston,* Hökerberg, 1928.
WEBSTER, JEAN, *Peters öden och äventyr,* Fahlcrantz, 1918.
—— *Unge Jerry,* Skoglund, 1918; *Jerry,* Holmquist, 1922; *Hennes vägvisare,* Kungsholmens bokhandel, 1932.
—— *Veteprinsessan,* Skoglund, 1918 (2 eds.).
—— *"Patty",* Skoglund, 1919 (3 eds.).
—— *Hemligheten på Four-Pools,* Skoglund, 1920; *Negerhyddans hemlighet,* Nordiska förlaget, 1922.
—— *Pappa Långben,* Åhlén & Åkerlund, 1916 (3 eds.); 1918, 1920; Bonnier, 1931, 1936.
—— *Patty och Priscilla,* Skoglund, 1921; Holmquist, 1922; *Pattys vidare öden,* Kungsholmens bokhandel, 1932, 1934.
—— *Pattys skoltid,* Holmquist, 1921; Kungsholmens bokhandel, 1932.
—— *"Min käraste fiende",* Skoglund, 1927 (2 eds.).
—— *Patty vid högskolan,* Bonnier, 1932.
WESTON, CHRISTINE, *Indigo,* Bonnier, 1945.
WHARTON, EDITH, *Glädjens hus,* Skoglund, 1922.
—— *Månstrålar,* Skoglund, 1923.
—— *Deras son,* Skoglund, 1924.
—— *Hans öde,* Skoglund, 1925.
—— *Lyckligt ogift,* Bonnier, 1929, 1930; Åhlén & Åkerlund, 1932.
—— *Den brutna linjen,* Bonnier, 1930.
—— *Barnen,* Bonnier, 1931.

WHIPPLE, MAURINE, *Löftets land,* Ljus, 1942.
WHITE, FRED M., *Den svartklädda damen,* B. Wahlström, 1916.
—— *Den blå damen,* Skoglund, 1917.
—— *Den gyllene rosen,* B. Wahlström, 1917.
—— *Den heliga orkidén,* B. Wahlström, 1918.
—— *Ett familjedrama,* Dahlberg, 1918.
—— *Mysteriet å Loudwater Priory,* Dahlberg, 1918.
—— *Charles Darrylls försvinnande,* B. Wahlström, 1919.
—— *Den svarta automobilen,* Nordiska förlaget, 1919.
—— *Ett spel om millioner,* B. Wahlström, 1922.
—— *Ebb och flod,* J. Zetterlund, 1923.
—— *Konspiratörer,* J. Zetterlund, 1923.
—— *Segerns vingar,* J. Zetterlund, 1923.
—— *Den röda triangeln,* J. Zetterlund, 1926.
—— *Huset vid spåret,* J. Zetterlund, 1926.
—— *Lady Amorys diamanter,* Halmstad, Hallandsposten, 1929.
WHITE, STEWART E., *Den långa resan,* Nutiden, 1917.
—— *Leopardkvinnan,* Bonnier, 1919.
—— *En karlakarl,* Holmquist, 1921.
—— *Nätter i Arizona,* Holmquist, 1922.
—— *Pälsjägaren,* Bonnier, 1923.
—— *Guld,* Bonnier, 1924.
—— *Floden,* Saxon & Lindström, 1939.
WHITE, WILLIAM L., *Det sägs i stan . . .,* Geber, 1939.
—— *Så dö drottningar,* Ljus, 1944.
WIDDEMAR, MARGARET, *Ett resonemangsparti,* Bonnier, 1920.
WIGGIN, KATE D., *Flickan från Amerika,* B. Wahlström, 1920.
WILDER, ISABEL, *Laura och barnen,* Skoglund, 1933.
WILDER, THORNTON, *San Luis bro,* Natur och Kultur, 1928; Åhlén & söner, 1933.
—— *Kabalan,* Natur och Kultur, 1929.
—— *Kvinnan från Andros,* Natur och Kultur, 1930.
—— *Till himlen går min väg,* Natur och Kultur, 1935.
WILLIAMS, BEN AMES, *Min är hämnden,* Forum, 1945.
WINSLOW, Thyra S., *Revyflickan,* Skoglund, 1928.
WINTHER, SOPHUS K., *Rot i ny jord,* Lindfors, 1943.
WOLFE, THOMAS, *Se hemåt, ängel!* Bonnier, 1932.
WOLFF, MARITTA M., *Nattskift,* Forum, 1945.
WOODS, WILLIAM H., *Mörkast före gryningen,* Hökerberg, 1943.
WRIGHT, HAROLD B., *Flydda dagar,* Thall & Carlsson, 1922.
—— *Helen från det gamla huset,* Thall & Carlsson, 1922.
—— *Skogarnas dotter,* Saxon & Lindström, 1943.
WRIGHT, RICHARD, *Son av sitt land,* Bonnier, 1943, 1944.

WRIGHT, WILLARD H. ("S. S. van Dine"), *Greenemysteriet,* Schildt, 1930; Lindqvist, 1939.

—— *Kanariemysteriet,* Schildt, 1930; Lindqvist, 1939.

—— *Skarabémysteriet,* Schildt, 1931; Lindqvist, 1939.

—— *Gardenmysteriet,* Fritze, 1936.

—— *Kasinomysteriet,* Fritze, 1937.

—— *Drakdammens hemlighet,* Bonnier, 1938.

YARDLEY, HERBERT O., *J-37, spionernas drottning,* Hökerberg, 1935.

Supplementary Bibliography:
Selected Criticism of American Fiction in Sweden

Only reviews and essays pertaining to American authors discussed or mentioned particularly in this book as significant in the Swedish acceptance of American literature during the 1920's are included in this bibliography. Reviews and essays on microfilm in the Library of the University of Pennsylvania (see Preface) are starred. Newspaper abbreviations are those commonly used in Sweden; see List of Abbreviations Used, p. 13.

ANDERSON, SHERWOOD:

*BOLANDER, CARL-AUGUST, "Sherwood Anderson," *DN*, June 7 and 8, 1928; *reprinted in *Ismer och dikt*, Stockholm, 1928, pp. 125–136.

*— "Redaktör Anderson, U. S. A.," *DN*, February 2, 1931.

*[ELGSTRÖM, ANNA LENAH], "Tre gula," *Soc. Dem.*, September 18, 1928.

*"FR., P.," "Mörkt skratt," *Folkets Dagblad*, June 9, 1928.

*GULLBERG, HJALMAR, "Amerikansk och fransk exotism." *SDS*, June 18, 1928.

*LANDQUIST, JOHN, "Sherwood Anderson," *Aftonbladet*, August 5, 1928.

*LUNDKVIST, ARTUR, "Mörkt skratt," *Arbetaren*, June 20, 1928.

*ÖSTERLING, ANDERS, "Sherwood Anderson," *SvD*, March 25, 1928; *reprinted in *Dagens gärning, tredje samlingen*, Stockholm, 1931, pp. 108–118.

*RABENIUS, OLOF, "Amerikanskt," *ST*, June 16, 1928.

*S[ÖDERHIEL]M, H[ENNING], "En amerikansk roman," *GHT*, July 6, 1928.

CATHER, WILLA:

*"ATTIS," "Nybyggarbarn och pioniärkvinna," *SvD*, October 22, 1939.

*BELFRAGE, SIXTEN, "En stor amerikansk författarinna," *Göteborgs-Posten*, May 21, 1932.

*BERG, RUBEN, "Willa Cathers nya roman," *DN*, April 11, 1926; *reprinted, slightly condensed, in *Aftonbladet*, November 20, 1927.

*ELGSTRÖM, ANNA LENAH, "Betydande amerikansk författarinna," *Soc. Dem.*, November 16, 1936.

*— "Skuggor ur det gångna," *Soc. Dem.*, September 27, 1940.

"ESQ.," "En bok om svenskarna i Amerika," *Stockholms Dagblad*, December 20, 1919.

*"G., A. L.," "Willa (Sibert) Cather: Hell, Banbrytare!" *Dagens Tidning*, February 3, 1920.

*GIEROW, KARL RAGNAR, "Pionjär," *NDA*, November 6, 1939.

*"GWEN" [ELSE KLEEN], "Amerikansk missroman," *ST*, November 9, 1927.

"L., G.," "En amerikansk bok om svenskar," *SvD*, September 28, 1920.

*"N., M.," "En amerikansk familjefar," *Göteborgs Morgonpost*, November 14, 1927.

"O—DH," "Villa [sic] Sibert Cather: *Lärksången*," *Svenska Morgonbladet*, December 8, 1920.

*ÖSTERLING, ANDERS, "Ormen och korset," *ST*, November 16, 1938.

DELL, FLOYD:

*B[OLANDER], C[ARL]-A[UGUST], "En underlig amerikan," *DN*, March 14, 1923.

*HOLMBERG, OLLE, "En modern andes biografi," *NDA*, December 16, 1922.

*KÄMPE, ALFRED, "Litteratur," *Folkets Dagblad Politiken*, January 2, 1923.

DREISER, THEODORE:

*BERG, RUBEN, "En amerikansk tragedi," *Aftonbladet*, November 23, 1927.

*BOLANDER, CARL-AUGUST, "'Romanens Hindenburg,'" *DN*, September 28, 1929.

*BÖÖK, FREDRIK, "Det amerikanska kulturproblemet," *SvD*, October 10, 1927, and *"En amerikansk tragedi," *SvD*, October 11, 1927; both *reprinted under title "Theodore Dreiser" in *Från fyra sekler*, Stockholm, 1928, pp. 245–263.

*ELGSTRÖM, ANNA LENAH, "Theodore Dreiser," *Soc. Dem.*, December 4, 1927.

*— "Finansmannen," *Soc. Dem.*, October 21, 1929.

*— "Ett 'geni' av Amerika," *Soc. Dem.*, June 30, 1936.

*— "Theodore Dreisers sista," *SDS*, April 8, 1947.

*"En ny Dreiser," *Ny Dag*, December 3, 1920.

*"F—M, K.," "Amerikanskt psyke," *Arbetaren*, November 14, 1928.

*FOGELQVIST, THORSTEN, "Modern amerikansk realism: I. Ett inledande radioföredrag," *DN*, October 17, 1930, "II. Theodore Dreiser, " *DN*, October 24 and 25, 1930. See also under Lewis, Sinclair.

*GULLBERG, HJALMAR, "Från Hoppets Port till Dödshuset," *SDS*, November 30, 1927.

*— "Flarn för vinden," *SDS*, October 15, 1928.

*HAGBERG, KNUT, "En amerikansk tragedi," *NDA*, October 8, 1927.

*H[OLMBER]G, O[LLE], "Tomheten," *DN*, September 22 and 23, 1928.

*JÖNSSON, GABRIEL, "En amerikansk 'Lykke-Per,'" *SDS*, September 17, 1936.

*"L., A.," "En storsvulen livsskildring från 70-talets U. S. A.," *SDS*, September 26, 1929.

*LÖFSTEDT, ANNIE, "Tre böcker av Theodore Dreiser," in *En kvinna om böcker*, Stockholm, 1932, pp. 87—102.

*LUNDKVIST, ARTUR, "En livstragedi i det moderna Amerika," *Arbetaren*, November 1, 1927.

—— "Dreiser looks at New York," *Fönstret*, no. 17 (August 23, 1930), pp. 7—8.

*ÖSTERLING, ANDERS, "Amerikanskt genomsnitt," *SvD*, October 4, 1928.

*— "Dreisers läroår," *SvD*, August 22, 1931.

*— "Dreisers sista roman," *ST*, May 12, 1947.

*SELANDER, STEN, "Ett stycke av Amerikas själ," *Stockholms Dagblad*, November 2, 1927.

*— "Dreisers sista roman," *SvD*, October 20, 1947.

*S[ÖDERHIEL]M, H[ENNING], "En amerikansk roman," *GHT*, November 4, 1927.

*— "Journalistminnen," *GHT*, January 27, 1930.

*— "Amerikanska kvinnoprofiler," *GHT*, April 29, 1930.

*— "Amerikanska profiler," *GHT*, December 30, 1930.

*— "Amerikanskt liv," *GHT*, August 19, 1931.

*— "Tre generationer," *GHT*, January 31, 1948.

*"V., S.," "En rovriddare," *Arbetet*, October 14, 1930.

GLASGOW, ELLEN:

*AHLGREN, STIG, "Själar lämnade åt sig själva," *SDS*, December 4, 1933.

*ANDHÉ, RUNE, "En prisroman om vår tids människor," *Göteborgs Morgonpost*, October 7, 1942.

*"... EL," "Tre amerikanska författarinnor," *Arbetet*, September 26, 1942.

*"H—G, K.," "Nutida engelskt familjeliv," *Göteborgs Morgonpost*, November 27, 1930.

*"N., V.," "En familjetragedi," *SvD*, September 10, 1942.

*"S—G, R.," "Amerikanskt vardagsliv," *SDS*, December 21, 1928.

*Ö[STERLING], A[NDERS], "Amerikansk prisroman," *ST*, September 24, 1942.

*S[ÖDERHIEL]M, H[ENNING], "En klok bok," *GHT*, June 12, 1943.

HERGESHEIMER, JOSEPH:

*BOLANDER, CARL-AUGUST, "Ny översättningslitteratur," *DN*, October 20, 1926.

*HOLMBERG, OLLE, "'Ammidons hus,'" *NDA*, May 1, 1921.

*"J., G.," "En artistisk amerikan," *SDS*, September 13, 1926.

*Röbbing, Lännart, "Joseph Hergesheimer," *Lunds Dagblad,* May 2, 1921.
*S[trömber]g, Kj[ell], "Exotisk frihetsromantik," *ST,* September 14, 1926.
*S[öderhiel]m, H[enning], "Kubansk romantik," *GHT,* August 26, 1926.
*"W., E. K.," "En amerikansk romantiker," *Lunds Dagblad,* September 13, 1926.

Lewis, Sinclair:

*"A—m, S.," "Avslöjad charlatan," *Aftontidningen,* April 3, 1945.
Abenius, Margit, "Ann Vickers och andra," *Bonniers Litterära Magasin,* II (March 1933), 61–66.
Ahlenius, Holger, "Sinclair Lewis' nya roman," *Morgontidningen,* July 2, 1934.
*Andersson, Elis, "Saken och kvinnan," *Göteborgs-Posten,* January 31, 1933.
*Attorps, Gösta, "Nobelpristagare," *SvD,* December 19, 1938.
"B., E.," "Grönköping i Newyork," *Göteborgs Morgonpost,* March 14, 1925.
*"B—n, B.," "En amerikansk diktaturdröm," *DN,* June 23, 1936.
Berg, Ruben, "En intressant amerikansk roman," *Aftonbladet,* December 5, 1921.
—— "En ny roman av Sinclair Lewis," *Aftonbladet,* December 20, 1923.
—— "Sinclair Lewis' senaste roman," *Aftonbladet,* September 10, 1926.
—— "En ny roman av Sinclair Lewis," *Aftonbladet,* October 24, 1929.
Bergstrand, Allan, "Babbitt," *Ny Tid,* March 6, 1924.
*"Bmn, B.," "Vanartiga föräldrar," *Morgontidningen;* February 4, 1939.
B[olander], C[arl]-A[ugust], "En amerikansk vardagshistoria," *DN,* November 26, 1924.
—— "En amerikansk läkarroman," *DN,* April 24, 1925.
—— "President Coolidges klasskamrat," *DN,* May 16, 1928.
—— "Mister Babbitt i Europa," *DN,* April 3, 1929.
Böök, Fredrik, "Babbitt," *SvD,* November 26, 1923.
—— "Amerikanskt," *SvD,* December 5, 1924.
—— "Sinclair Lewis," *SvD,* April 15, 22, and 29, 1928.
—— "En ny Sinclair Lewis," *SvD,* June 4, 1928.
—— "Amerikaner i Europa," *SvD,* April 2, 1929.
*—— "Ann Vickers," *SvD,* February 14, 1933.
*—— "En ny Sinclair Lewis," *SvD,* February 5, 1934.
*—— "Fascistisk revolution i U. S. A.," *SvD,* February 3, 1936.
*—— "En ny Sinclair Lewis," *SvD,* March 26, 1945.
*Borglund, Harry, "Litteraturkritik ur befordringssynpunkt," *Ny Tid,* February 25, 1928.
*Ekström, Kjell, "Ny bok av Lewis," *SDS,* November 24, 1944.
*—— "Sinclair Lewis' senaste bok," *SDS,* July 18, 1946.
*Elgström, Anna Lenah, "En pånyttfödd Sinclair Lewis," *Soc. Dem.,* May 13, 1933.

*ERDMANN, NILS, "Den amerikanska kvinnan," NDA, September 9, 1933.

*— "Om hotellmän," NDA, October 4, 1934.

—— "Sinclair Lewis framtidsbild av amerikansk nazism," NDA, July 9, 1936.

F[OGELQVIS]T, T[ORSTEN], "Nytt från Zenith," DN, November 28, 1928.

—— "Modern amerikansk realism: I. Ett inledande radioföredrag," DN, October 17, 1930, "III. Sinclair Lewis," DN, October 31, November 1, 1930. See also under Dreiser, Theodore.

*— "Nobelpristagare berättar historier," DN, November 1, 1937.

GREVENIUS, HERBERT, "Flirten med vildmarken," Stockholms Dagblad, February 12, 1927.

*— "Kvinnan i vingården," ST, January 29, 1933.

"GWEN" [ELSE KLEEN], "En bra roman," ST, October 23, 1925.

*HAGBERG, KNUT, "Sinclair Lewis som religionskritiker," NDA, February 19, 1928.

HALLSTRÖM, PER, "Två romaner av Babbitts författare," SvD, December 19, 1925.

*HELLSTRÖM, GUSTAF, "Föräldrar och barn," DN, March 21, 1938.

*— "Tvillingsystrar," DN, October 23, 1941.

*H[OLMBER]G, O[LLE], "Sinclair Lewis nya bok," DN, February 27, 1933.

*— "Konstverk och livets verk," DN, June 11, 1934.

"J., G.," "En kritik av Amerika," SvD, December 22, 1921.

*JOHNSON, EYVIND, "Sinclair Lewis nya roman — ett jättereportage," Arbetet, February 3, 1933.

*JOHNSSON, MELKER, "Amerikansk självprövning," Ny Tid, April 5, 1928.

*JÖNSSON, GABRIEL, "Noveller av Sinclair Lewis," SDS, October 13, 1937.

*J[ONSSO]N, T[HORSTEN], "En droppe negerblod," DN, May 27, 1947.

"L., H. W.," 'Storstadsbon i vildmarken," Göteborgs Morgonpost, April 7, 1927.

—— "En amerikansk kontorsflicka," Göteborgs Morgonpost, October 27, 1927.

*LAGERCRANTZ, OLOF, "Sinclair Lewis' nya roman," SvD, January 31, 1946.

LANDQUIST, JOHN, "En amerikansk läkarroman," Aftonbladet, June 17, 1926.

*LARSSON, AXEL, "Sinclair Lewis' nya skarpa samhällssatir," SDS, October 17, 1929.

"LBK, ARNE," "Sinclair Lewis: Falkens bana," Östgöta Correspondenten, November 24, 1925.

*LUNDKVIST, ARTUR, "Ulv i fårakläder," Arbetaren, February 20, 1928.

*— "Streber i helfigur," ST, April 9, 1945.

MÖLLER, BERT, "Sinclair Lewis," Biblioteksbladet, Organ för Sveriges biblioteksförening, XIV (1929), 1—7.

"N., V.," "En droppe negerblod," SvD, May 27, 1947.

NYLÉN, EINAR, "Det moderna Amerika," Göteborgs Aftonblad, December 21, 1923.

NYMAN, THURE, "Americana," Bonniers Litterära Magasin, III (June 1934), 80—81.

OLJELUND, IVAN, "Brevkort från Sinclair Lewis," SvD, September 26, 1937.

OLSSON, BROR, "Sinclair Lewis," NDA, June 6, 1928.

OLSSON, GUSTAF, "Sinclair Lewis och kalvinismen," NDA, April 7, 1927.

*ÖSTERLING, ANDERS, "Diktatur i U. S. A.," ST, June 6, 1936.

P[AULI], I[VAN], "Sinclair Lewis: En märklig amerikansk samhällsskildrare," *Arbetet*, February 27, 1924.

—— "Amerikanskt," *Arbetet*, December 29, 1925.

—— "Själasörjaren från Kansas," *Soc. Dem.*, March 25, 1928.

—— "Han som kände Coolidge," *Soc. Dem.*, June 5, 1928.

—— "Dodsworth, kvinnan och Europa," *Soc. Dem.*, May 22, 1929.

*—— "Vanartiga föräldrar," *Soc. Dem.*, December 21, 1938.

*PIHL, GUNNAR T., "Fascistdiktatur i U. S. A.," *SDS*, May 23, 1936.

*ROGBERG, MARTIN, "Reporter bakom kulisserna," *SvD*, April 20, 1940.

*RUNNQUIST, ÅKE, "Välgörenhetens humbug," *NDA*, July 8, 1944.

S[EGERSTEDT], T[ORGNY], "En amerikansk boksuccès," *GHT*, April 12, 1922.

*SELANDER, STEN, "U. S. A:s samvete," *Stockholms Dagblad*, August 15, 1927.

S[ÖDERHIEL]M, H[ENNING], "Amerikansk nutid," *GHT*, April 17, 1925.

—— "Falkens bana," *GHT*, March 9, 1926.

—— "Äventyr i vildmarken," *GHT*, September 1, 1926.

—— "En ny roman av Sinclair Lewis," *GHT*, April 7, 1927.

*—— "Sinclair Lewis' nya bok," *GHT*, May 26, 1928.

*—— "Sinclair Lewis' nya roman," *GHT*, March 25, 1929.

*—— "En ny roman av Sinclair Lewis," *GHT*, January 23, 1934.

*—— "En protest mot våldet," *GHT*, November 8, 1935.

*—— "Noveller av Sinclair Lewis," *GHT*, September 28, 1937.

*—— "Sinclair Lewis' senaste," *GHT*, July 5, 1940.

*—— "En charlatan," *GHT*, May 2, 1944.

*—— "Amerikanska äktenskap," *GHT*, June 28, 1946.

*—— "En martyr," *GHT*, August 20, 1947.

STRAND, SVEN G., "Amerikanskt," *Soc. Dem.*, July 19, 1927.

STRÖMBERG, KJELL, "Sinclair Lewis och problemet Amerika," *Ord och Bild*, XL (1931), 153—161.

*SVENSSON, GEORG, "Mannen som Babbitt ville lära känna," *NDA*, March 20, 1929.

*"V., S.," "Elmer Gantry," *Arbetet*, March 1, 1928.

*"W—s, I.," "Amerikanska romaner," *DN*, March 25, 1945.

WERIN, ALGOT, "Lycko-Per i Amerika," *SDS*, June 3, 1926.

LONDON, JACK:

*"A., A—a," "Jack London och hans diktargärning," *SvD*, August 20, 1920.

*"E., H.," "Bland böcker: Jack London," *Dagen*, September 28, 1915.

*ERIKSSON, BROR, "Litteratur: Jack London," *Östgöten*, September 21, 1917.

*—— "Jack London och hans diktargärning," *Svenska Morgonbladet*, June 8, 1920.

*—— "Jack London som dramatiker," *Östgöten*, October 20, 1920.

ENGHOLM, STELLAN, "Jack London," *Frihet*, no. 2 (1919), pp. 2—3.

*—— "Jack London: en överblick," *Politiken*, August 30, 1919.

—— "Naturfilosofi," *Frihet*, no. 3 (1920), pp. 5—6.

*"J—N, C.," "Litteratur: Jack London," *Soc. Dem.*, June 5, 1914.

*"JENKI," "Järnhälen," *Verdandisten*, June 12, 1913.

*KÄMPE, ALFR[ED], "Litteratur: En Hawaji-bok av Jack London," *Folkets Dagblad Politiken*, November 11, 1922.

*KOCH, MARTIN, "'Kungen av Klondyke,'" *Ny Tid*, January 3, 1914.

*"L., C.," "Litteratur," *Signalen*, April 22, 1920.

*"Litteratur: Jack London," *Soc. Dem.*, December 5, 1914.

*LUNDBORG, OSKAR, "'Klasskamp och revolution,'" *Politiken*, April 5, 1919.

*MAGNUS-CARLSSON, AXEL, "Litteratur: Jack London," *Östergötlands Folkblad*, April 27, 1917.

*MÖRNER, BIRGER, "Kring Jack London," *Södermanlands Läns Tidning*, July 1, 1922.

*NORDSTRAND, G., "Jack Londons sista bok," *NDA*, December 22, 1922.

*"R—S, O.," "Ny berättelsesamling af Jack London, *Stockholms Dagblad*, September 18, 1915.

*"RBG," "Bokvärlden: Jack London," *GHT*, November 19, 1914.

*"S., O.," "Litteratur: Kungen av Klondyke," *Soc. Dem.*, December 20, 1913.

*"S—M, B.," "En bok om Jack London," *Lunds Dagblad*, May 8, 1920.

POOLE, ERNEST:

*ROSEN, SVEN, "Modern amerikansk romankonst," *Stockholms Dagblad*, January 9, 1916.

SINCLAIR, UPTON:

*AHLBERG, ALF, "I dårarnas paradis," *DN*, December 6, 1945.

*B[ERGER], S[VEN], "Är 1939 enligt Upton Sinclair," *SDS*, December 9, 1946.

*B[LOMBERG], H[ARRY], "En bok om krig och socialism," *Nya Norrland*, April 10, 1920.

*BRANDELL, GUNNAR, "Politik och spiritism," *GHT*, December 10, 1945.

*"H—N, ER[IK], "Den Store Amerikanen," *Soc. Dem.*, July 29, 1921.

*— "Upton Sinclair: Kung Kol," *Soc. Dem.*, May 23, 1923.

*— "Böcker: En väldig social roman," *Politiken*, May 25, 1918.

*— "Upton Sinclairs väldigaste bok," *Soc. Dem.*, December 24, 1919.

HEDENVIND-ERIKSSON, GUSTAV, "Upton Sinclair," *Frihet*, no. 14 (Christmas 1921), pp. 3, 4, 10.

KEY, ELLEN, "Upton Sinclair och freden," *Frihet*, no. 10 (1918), pp. 3—4.

*LUNDQVIST, ERNEST J., "Litteratur: Upton Sinclair," *Signalen*, December 7, 1917.

*"NIDOLV," "Jack London och den amerikanska pressen," *Västsvenska Kuriren*, January 22, 1921.

*Persson, Edvin E., "Ny jättevolym av Sinclair," *Ny Dag*, December 6, 1946.
*Rosén, Arvid, "I samhällets inferno och långt bortom," *Ny Tid*, September 18, 1925.

Wharton, Edith:

*Attorps, Gösta, "En amerikansk författarinna," *SvD*, September 26, 1930.
*Böök, Fredrik, "Typen Pauline Manford," *SvD*, November 11, 1929.
*— "Edith Whartons roman," *SvD*, November 18, 1929.
*Elgström, Anna Lenah, "Edith Wharton," *Soc. Dem.*, December 23, 1929.
*Erdmann, Nils, "Från Amerika," *NDA*, October 8, 1930.
*F[ogelqvis]t, T[orsten], "Amerikansk sedesatir," *DN*, November 6, 1921.
*H[olmber]g, O[lle], "Det förflutna," *DN*, September 8, 1930.
*L[öfste]dt, A[nnie], "Mrs. Manford från U. S. A.," *GHT*, November 29, 1929;
    *reprinted in *En kvinna om böcker*, Stockholm, 1932, pp. 103—107.
*Österling, Anders, "Edith Whartons minnen," *SvD*, June 30, 1934.
*Stjernstedt, Marika, "Societetstragedi," *SvD*, June 3, 1921.
*"V., S.," "En patricisk författarinna," *Arbetet*, October 29, 1930.

Holdings in and Circulation of American Fiction in Twenty-Two Swedish Lending Libraries, 1951

In order to supplement the information concerning the course of American fiction in Sweden contained in the text and in Appendix A of the present study, which stress the critical reception of that literature and the publication record respectively, a survey was undertaken in 1951 of the holdings in and circulation of American fiction in Swedish lending libraries throughout the country. Because of the very active use made of such libraries in Sweden, the results of the survey, which appear on the following pages, are a valuable index to public interest in American fiction and particularly to relative interest in individual authors. Questionnaires with a list of 112 authors, chosen on the basis of reputed popularity, active translation of their work, or contemporaneity in the period of interest, were sent to thirty libraries suggested as representative of varying social conditions in Sweden by *förste bibliotekskonsulent* Bengt Hjelmqvist, whose department in Skolöverstyrelsen had recently completed a similar study for Swedish authors. Of the thirty, eight libraries (those in Falun, Gävle, Kiruna, Landskrona, Lidingö, Lidköping, Norrköping, and Västerås) did not reply, and one, the Central Library in Stockholm, was able only to furnish data that could not be incorporated in the general survey; excerpts from the Stockholm reply are given following the general survey.

The twenty-one reporting libraries are listed below in column (1) with figures showing: in column (2), the total number of books by the authors named in the questionnaire owned by the library in translation; column (3), the total number of such books in circulation as of March 12, 1951 (April 2 for Karlstad); column (4), the total number of books by the authors named in the questionnaire owned by the library in the original language; and column (5), the total number of such books in circulation as of March 12, 1951 (April 2 for Karlstad):

Combined totals, by library, of holdings in and circulation of
selected American fiction in twenty-one Swedish libraries
as of March 12, 1951.

Library	In translation		In original	
	No. vols.	Vols. on loan	No. vols.	Vols. on loan
1	2	3	4	5
Borås	433	280	154	27
Eskilstuna	750	480	195	45
Göteborg (Dicksonska)	1,035	909	322	178
Halmstad	386	154	181	21
Hälsingborg	637	235	330	36
Huskvarna	326	131	32	4
Jönköping	448	307	141	61
Kalmar	723	324	144	31
Karlskoga	596	292	118	35
Karlskrona	697	365	111	23
Karlstad	374	18	148	0
Kristianstad	576	148	158	30
Linköping	381	289	139	50
Lund	505	279	87	34
Malmö	3,967	1,734	484	142
Örebro	1,343	505	278	52
Östersund	592	130	145	13
Sundsvall	405	171	60	12
Umeå	508	353	97	29
Uppsala	524	244	357	87
Visby	271	155	71	6
Totals	15,477	7,503	3,752	916

Combined totals, by author, of holdings in and circulation of
selected American fiction in twenty-one Swedish libraries
as of March 12, 1951.

	In translation		In original	
Author	No. vols.	Vols. on loan	No. vols.	Vols. on loan
1	2	3	4	5
Alcott, Louisa	202	68	17	5
Algren, Nelson	12	6	3	1
Allen, Hervey	244	115	45	5
Allen, James Lane	12	0	4	1
Anderson, Sherwood	37	10	19	1
Atherton, Gertrude	4	0	8	1
Baldwin, Faith	22	10	5	2
Bartlett, Frederick	6	2	0	0
Beach, Rex	39	15	18	0
Bellamann, Henry	48	28	2	1
Bellamy, Edward	17	0	1	0
Biggers, Earl D.	80	48	4	1
Bristow, Gwen	194	108	15	7
Bromfield, Louis	583	368	172	56
Buck, Pearl	939	582	221	72
Burnett, Frances H.	173	53	23	6
Burroughs, Edgar R.	23	14	58	12
Cabell, James B.	17	8	9	3
Cain, James M.	51	37	30	8
Caldwell, Erskine	149	93	79	29
Caldwell, Taylor	120	64	51	14
Carr, John D.	173	131	34	16
Cather, Willa	351	100	115	31
Clark, Walter V. T.	45	35	13	2
Clemens, Samuel L.	650	313	67	14
Cooper, J. Fenimore	412	242	25	1
Costain, Thomas B.	96	65	23	7
Crane, Stephen	0	0	5	1
Crawford, F. Marion	19	0	14	1
Curwood, James O.	301	153	30	6
Dana, Richard H.	15	5	3	1
Davenport, Marcia	60	38	10	5
Davis, Richard H.	2	1	7	0
Day, Clarence	76	26	28	8
Dell, Floyd	9	3	6	0
Disney, Dorothy	95	79	8	5

(Continued)

1	2	3	4	5
Dos Passos, John	87	30	39	5
Douglas, Lloyd C.	37	14	9	4
Dreiser, Theodore	388	141	82	11
Du Bois, Theodora	122	96	1	1
Edmonds, Walter D.	101	47	16	2
Farrell, James T.	49	32	47	13
Fast, Howard	85	33	25	8
Faulkner, William	196	158	89	54
Ferber, Edna	207	82	98	17
Field, Rachel	96	48	24	9
Fitzgerald, F. Scott	27	11	13	6
Gardner, Erle S.	80	60	30	11
Garland, Hamlin	0	0	1	0
Glasgow, Ellen	73	26	14	1
Gold, Michael	20	6	0	0
Grey, Zane	22	13	27	3
Gunter, Archibald	61	2	6	0
Hammett, Dashiell	36	26	15	8
Harte, Bret	86	4	65	4
Hawthorne, Nathaniel	40	9	26	3
Hearn, Lafcadio	70	6	15	0
Hemingway, Ernest	230	149	110	43
Hergesheimer, Joseph	80	11	48	4
Herrick, Robert	7	0	3	0
Hersey, John	93	62	15	7
Heyward, DuBose	17	3	6	2
Hill, Grace L.	0	0	0	0
Hobson, Laura Z.	52	40	9	3
Howells, William D.	1	0	1	0
Hurst, Fannie	81	11	25	1
Irving, Washington	48	8	25	7
James, Henry	52	17	26	11
Keyes, Francis P.	89	70	15	9
Kyne, Peter B.	187	86	29	4
Lewis, Sinclair	751	277	251	42
Lewisohn, Ludwig	209	21	30	4
Lockridge, Ross	30	20	3	0
London, Jack	1,497	557	163	22
McCullers, Carson	89	34	13	4
Mailer, Norman	54	44	11	9
Marquand, John P.	271	133	35	11
Mason, F. Van Wyck	28	22	5	0
Melville, Herman	110	66	12	3

(Continued)

1	2	3	4	5
Mitchell, Margaret	155	102	27	3
Mowery, William B.	4	2	0	0
Nathan, Robert	33	5	9	3
Nordhoff and Hall	376	216	81	20
Norris, Frank	37	4	10	0
Norris, Kathleen	22	4	12	1
O'Hara, Mary	207	139	22	6
Ostenso, Martha	29	7	5	0
Poe, Edgar A.	126	68	44	9
Porter, William S.	23	3	23	2
Queen, Ellery	116	86	95	41
Rawlings, Marjorie	98	33	20	1
Reid, Mayne	49	12	5	0
Rinehart, Mary R.	89	48	5	0
Roberts, Kenneth L.	239	158	66	12
Schulberg, Budd	23	15	6	1
Sinclair, Upton	967	456	65	10
Smith, Lillian E.	66	63	42	4
Steinbeck, John	473	315	156	71
Stone, Irving	141	95	15	1
Stowe, Harriet B.	141	80	16	3
Tarkington, Booth	59	10	36	0
Terhune, Albert P.	94	38	6	1
Van Vechten, Carl	10	3	6	0
Wallace, Lew	53	21	7	0
Webster, Jean	213	81	51	12
Wharton, Edith	151	22	71	4
White, Stewart E.	11	4	8	0
Wilder, Thornton	165	28	59	11
Wolfe, Thomas	24	3	26	3
Wright, Richard	90	64	28	11
Wright, Willard	35	10	38	8
Totals	15,477	7,503	3,752	916

Totals, by author, of holdings in and circulation of American fiction in the Central Library of Stockholm as of May 21, 1951.

Note.—For two reasons the results of the survey of holdings in and circulation of American fiction in the Central Library in Stockholm, the largest lending library in Sweden, could not be incorporated in the reports from other libraries given in the preceding pages: (1) the impossibility of the Stockholm system to account reliably for many authors rendered the reported figures for those authors useless, and to have included the remaining authors in the general survey would have necessitated so many qualifications as to seriously vitiate the usefulness of that survey; (2) the Stockholm survey was not undertaken until May 21, 1951, when seasonal reading habits in Sweden may be expected to have changed greatly since March 12, when the other libraries reported, thus complicating still further the qualifications necessary if the Stockholm figures had been included. By themselves, however, these figures are valuable in suggesting the nature of the interest in American fiction in the capital city.

Author	In translation		In orginal	
	No. vols.	vols. on loan	No. vols.	Vols. on loan
1	2	3	4	5
Alcott, Louisa M.	271	43	14	2
Allen, Hervey	191	60	23	7
Bromfield, Louis	376	274	79	45
Buck, Pearl	616	414	99	32
Burnett, Frances H.	254	45	38	12
Cain, James M.	17	17	18	8
Caldwell, Erskine	75	66	43	19
Caldwell, Taylor	57	34	24	13
Cather, Willa	188	50	55	20
Curwood, James O.	383	167	8	2
Day, Clarence	69	27	17	5
Dos Passos, John	74	30	21	10
Dreiser, Theodore	328	131	43	21
Farrell, James T.	15	15	29	8
Faulkner, William	128	111	45	39
Ferber, Edna	149	82	34	16
Fitzgerald, F. Scott	7	10	12	7
Glasgow, Ellen	62	17	10	1
Hemingway, Ernest	164	129	58	36
Hergesheimer, Joseph	48	11	35	1
Hurst, Fannie	63	28	24	4
Kyne, Peter B.	204	109	16	2
Lewisohn, Ludwig	85	19	19	1
Lockridge, Ross	18	15	2	1
London, Jack	1,224	509	104	15
Marquand, John P.	58	34	19	7
Melville, Herman	88	50	11	3
Nordhoff and Hall	205	116	36	8
Poe, Edgar A.	77	48	19	3
Steinbeck, John	235	172	78	42
Stowe, Harriet B.	68	39	7	1
Tarkington, Booth	55	17	35	3
Wharton, Edith	115	42	46	5
Wilder, Thornton	76	15	22	6
Wolfe, Thomas	21	6	15	5
Wright, Richard	24	22	9	1

INDEX

Agrell, Sigurd, 31–32, 86
Alcott, Louisa May, 34
America
  a world power, 15, 64
  British criticism of, 17–18
  Swedish attitude toward, 10, 15; favorable in 18th & 19th cent., 15–17; thereafter regarding A. as a threat, menace, etc., 17, 18, 46, 47, 48, 55, 86, 93; as a "standardized" civilization, 24, 33, 46, 47, 48–50, 53, 57, 63, 72, 73, 76, and *passim;* as smug, overbearing, etc., 19, 22, 24, 25, 30, 36, 57, 63, 76, 86, and *passim;* as culturally deficient, 20, 22, 27, 28–29, 33, 36 n., 46, 47, 49–50 51, 56, 57, 86, and *passim;* as materialistic, 19, 21–22, 26, 27, 30, 36 n., 46, 47, 63, 75–76, 86, and *passim*
  Swedish criticism of: for attitude toward women, 28, 30, 39, 40, 62, 74; for capitalism, 28, 30, 48; for failure to fuse motley population, 23, 32, 33; for hostility toward labor, 30; for inadequacies of the press, 20, 28, 30; for plight of the Negro, 27, 28, 30
  Swedish emigration to, 16, 17, 26
American literature, reputation in Sweden of:
  favorable though slight in 18th & 19th cent., 15–17; reversed by Hamsun, 20–23, and by Hellström, 28–29; not improved by popular successes of London & Sinclair, 36, 44; improved by critical as well as popular successes of Lewis, 45, 51–52, 56–57, 62–63, and of his contemporaries, 64–67, 71, 81–83; crowned by 1930 Nobel Prize, 85–87; concerned thereafter with literary qualities, 94, 97
  SEE ALSO Drama, Fiction, Poetry, and under individual American authors
Anderson, Sherwood, 66, 67, 70, 71–73, 81, 87–88, 92, 96, 97, 98
Andersson, Dan, 43
Angered-Strandberg, Hilma, 31
Atherton, Gertrude, 34
Bailey, Temple, 67
Bellamy, Edward, 34
Berg, Ruben, 46, 48, 52–54, 56, 61, 66, 69, 82
Berger, Henning, 23, 25–26, 59 n., 63, 83, 85, 86
Bergman, Hjalmar, 32, 86
Björkman, Edwin, 19 n.
Björnson, Björnstjerne, 19 n.
Blomberg, Harry, 42
Böök, Fredrik, 24–25, 25–26, 48–50, 51, 56, 60–61, 62, 74, 76, 77, 78, 80
Bohlin & Co., 37
Bolander, Carl-August, 56
Bremer, Fredrika, 15, 16, 34
Bromfield, Louis, 82, 110
Brooks, Van Wyck, 87
Buck, Pearl, 99, 110
Burnett, Frances H., 34
Burroughs, Edgar R., 67
Cabell, James Branch, 92
Cable, George W., 35
Cather, Willa, 66, 67, 69–70, 82, 91, 92